D0520957

The Little Hands BIG FUN CRAFT BOOK

By Judy Press

Illustrated by
Loretta Trezzo Braren

williamsonbooks™

Nashville, Tennessee

ISBN-13: 978-0-8249-6827-4 (softcover)
ISBN-13: 978-0-8249-6826-7 (hardcover)

Published by Williamson Books
An imprint of Ideals Publications
A Guideposts Company
Nashville, Tennessee
www.idealsbooks.com

Printed and bound in the USA

Library of Congress Cataloging-in-Publication Data
Press, Judy, 1944–
    the little hands big fun craft book: creative fun for 2- to 6-
year-olds / Judy Press
    p. cm.—(A Williamson little hands book; 3)
    Includes index.
    Summary: Presents over seventy-five simple arts and crafts
activities related to holidays, school, occupations, travel,
nature, home, and friendship.
    1. Handicraft—Juvenile literature. 2. Creative activities and
seatwork—Juvenile literature. 3. Early childhood education-
Activity programs—Juvenile literature. [1. Handicraft.]
I. Title. II. Series
TT160.P782 1995
745.5—dc20   95-17574
                              CIP
                              AC

Illustrations by: Loretta Trezzo Braren
Designed by: Georgina Chidlow-Rucker

Little Hands® and Kids Can® are registered trademarks of
Ideals Publications.

RRD-Wil_Aug10_2

• •

Dedication

This book is dedicated to the women of 1314:
Nona, Clara, Esther, Lena, and Annie.

PARENTS'
CHOICE
APPROVED

• •

Contents

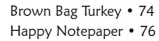

A Word to Grownups & Kids • 5

Animals & Trees • 7
Earth Day Crown • 8
Sewing Card Tree • 10
Sawdust Bugs • 12
Fantastic Footprints • 14
Sock Puppet Pet • 16
Four Season Trees • 18

School Days • 19
Noodle Nametag • 20
Apple Print Book Bag • 22
Sandpaper Letter Rubbings • 24
Color Match Game • 26
Sparkling Shapes Mobile • 28
Cereal Counter • 30
Cookie Sheet Clock • 32
Weather Watch Board • 34
Polka-Dot Lunch Bag • 36

Big Fun Crafts • 37
Bottle Bowling Pins • 38
Bobbing Boat • 40
Pie Tin Wind Chime • 42
Cardboard Carton Storage Cart • 44
Picture Puzzle • 46
Cardboard Box Bookshelves • 48
Tray Sailboat • 50

Family Fun • 51
"All About Me" Scrapbook • 52
Handprint Family Tree • 54
"We're So Proud!" Medal • 56
Hearts & Flowers Necklace • 58
Stocking Finger Puppet • 60
Cozy Kitty Pillow • 62
Tooth Fairy Pouch • 64

Friendship • 65
Friendship Paper Quilt • 66
Love Plant • 68
Tea Party Placemat • 70
Friendship Bracelets • 72

Brown Bag Turkey • 74
Happy Notepaper • 76

Around-the-World Celebrations • 77
America: Yankee Doodle Dandy Headband • 78
Egypt: Crackled Egg Art • 80
Israel: Shoebox Sukkah • 82
Japan: Stuffed Paper Fish • 84
China: Paper Bag Dragon • 86
Nigeria: Oatmeal Canister Drum • 88
India: Floating Diwali Candle • 90
Vietnam: Swinging Lantern • 92
England: Pressed Flower Card • 94
Canada: Sponge Print Gift Wrap • 96
Italy: Berry Basket Cricket House • 98
Mexico: Seed Shaker Maraca • 100
Brazil: Peek-a-Boo Carnival Mask • 102

Neighborhood • 103
Ghostly Sponge Prints • 104
Paper Bag Mail Pouch • 106
Paper Plate Stop Sign • 108
Foil Mirror Headband • 110
"Open Wide" Paper Bag Puppet • 112

Outdoor Fun • 113
Cardboard Carton Obstacle Course • 114
Flashlight Fun • 116
Picnic Pack • 118
Egg Carton Seed Starter • 120
Bubble Prints • 122
Rainbow Snow • 124

Big Fun in Special Places • 125
The Zoo: Zany Zoo Animals • 126
The Museum: Fancy Frame • 128
The Circus: Straw Acrobat • 130
The Beach: Seashell Paperweight • 132
The Library: Photo Bookmark • 134
The Farm: Old MacDonald Mural • 136
The Aquarium: Paper Plate Fish Tank • 138

Index • 140

Acknowledgments

Having earned a B.F.A. in Art Education from Syracuse University and an M.Ed. in Art Education from the University of Pittsburgh, I would like to acknowledge both schools for their dedication to the arts and to teacher education. I have found teaching art to be immensely satisfying, and I feel privileged to have taught art to many children and adults in the greater-Pittsburgh area.

I would like to thank the following for their support and encouragement in the writing of this book: my neighbor Cory Polena; the Mt. Lebanon Public Library; Andrea Perry; Carol Baicker-Mckee; the Children's Book Writing Group of Mt. Lebanon; my husband, Allan; and my children, Brian, Debbie, Darren, and Matt.

This book would not have been possible without the talent and dedication of the following people at Williamson Publishing: Susan and Jack Williamson, Jennifer Ingersoll, Judy Raven, June Roelle, Jennifer Adkisson, and the creative talent of Ken Braren and Loretta Trezzo Braren.

A Word to Grownups & Kids

This is a book that celebrates family and friends, national and international holidays, trips, and special events. It suggests craft projects, games to play, books to read, gifts to make, and both indoor and outdoor activities. It incorporates a concept of whole learning that will  entertain and inform children and grownups.

The materials needed to complete the projects in this book are readily available, and the directions are direct and easy to follow. Many of the materials are recycled paper products and packaging materials that would otherwise end up in landfills. Each craft can be embellished in the unique way a child chooses. Have the following supplies on hand before you begin: child safety scissors, white craft glue, tape, package of assorted colors of construction paper, newspaper, shirt cardboard, poster paints in primary colors, a paintbrush, markers, a hole punch, and a stapler.

Craft projects can be created from many of the things we discard, so be an industrious scavenger. Keep a box on hand to save the following: fabric scraps and trim, foil paper, colorful wrapping paper, paper plates and cups, cardboard tubes, Popsicle sticks, dried plant material, seashells, Styrofoam trays (from non-meat products only), cardboard boxes, string, and yarn.

As a general rule of safety, always do art in a well-ventilated room, assess your young crafter's propensity to put small objects in his or her mouth (make appropriate materials decisions accordingly), and work with nontoxic materials. Keep in mind that younger  siblings may pick up odds and ends from the floor or pull items off the table's edge.

Most items used in these projects can be handled safely by little hands. Where scissors are used, please use child safety scissors— **never adult sharp scissors**. It is worth investing in a pair of good child safety scissors

that can really cut. Cutting is a skill that children develop slowly, so allow them to practice their cutting skills on scraps of paper, and be ready to help if your child is not yet ready to cut with scissors.

Assess your child's readiness when using tools such as staplers and hole punches too. To prevent any accidents or injuries, very young children should not work directly with these tools. When helping young children, always ask, "Where would you like me to cut?" so the young artist maintains creative control of his or her own project.

When using recycled Styrofoam trays, use only those that contained fruits or vegetables or other non-meat items such as nuts. Meat trays, even after washing, may still contain traces of contaminants from uncooked meat. If fruit and vegetable Styrofoam trays aren't available to recycle, use a pie tin, piece of cardboard, or heavy paper plate.

Although specific instructions are provided in the book in order to complete a project, remember to allow a child to make choices whenever possible. It is not necessary for crafts to take an exact shape or form; instead, encourage new ideas, designs, and individualized interpretations. In a group, each craft should stand out as different from the rest. A grownup can determine if a younger child may need assistance.

The crafts in this book can be created at special times or for anytime. Memorable times are treasured by each of us, and the sharing of time and space and creative energy are often

what children grow to cherish. Through arts, crafts, and celebrations, we can share in the joy of being together in a relaxed atmosphere, where a good time can be had by all who participate. Keep an open mind when crafting with young children, and remember that the experience of creating together is more important than a finished product.

•   •   •

Animals & Trees

Earth Day Crown

Our Earth's a special planet
That spins around the sun;
Keep it clean and treat it well—
It's home to everyone!

Here's What You Need

- **Construction paper (assorted colors including green)**
- **Child safety scissors**
- **White craft glue**
- **Stapler**

Here's What You Do

1 Cut green construction paper 8³/4" x 24" (22 cm x 60 cm). Cut long, pointed triangles around the paper.

2 Cut flowers, butterflies, trees, fish, sun clouds, and birds from assorted colors of construction paper. Glue onto points of crown, and let dry completely.

3 Wrap crown around head, and staple crown edges together.

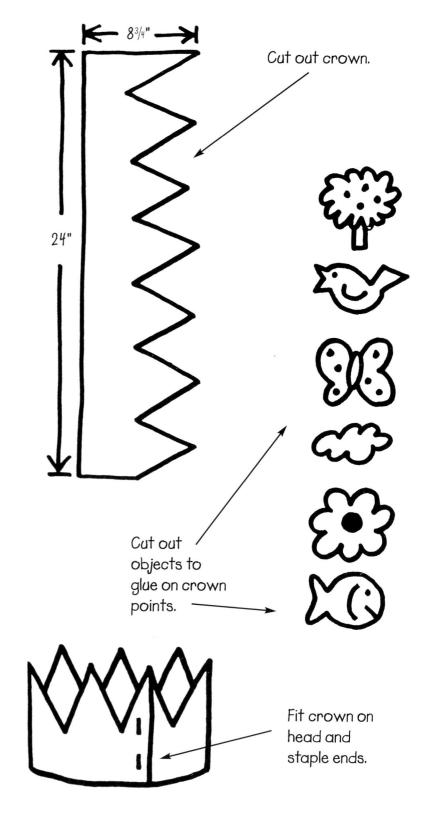

← 8³/4" →

24"

Cut out crown.

Cut out objects to glue on crown points.

Fit crown on head and staple ends.

Finished Earth
Day Crown

MORE BIG FUN!

★ Look closely at the things we throw
away. Can you think of a way to
use them again?

★ In a box, save things such
as seashells, shiny ribbon,
pretty paper, old
greeting cards, fabric
scraps, and yarn. Then
recycle them in art
projects.

★ Make a list of things you can
do to save the Earth. Then
ask your family for help.

Sewing Card Tree

*We celebrate Arbor Day
As they did years ago—
Planting lots of young, new trees,
And watching as they grow!*

Here's What You Need

- **Shirt cardboard**
- **Markers**
- **Child safety scissors**
- **Hole punch**
- **Yarn**

Here's What You Do

1 Draw the shape of a tree on the cardboard. Cut it out, then punch holes around the tree.

2 Color the tree, then sew through holes with yarn.

Draw tree shape on cardboard.

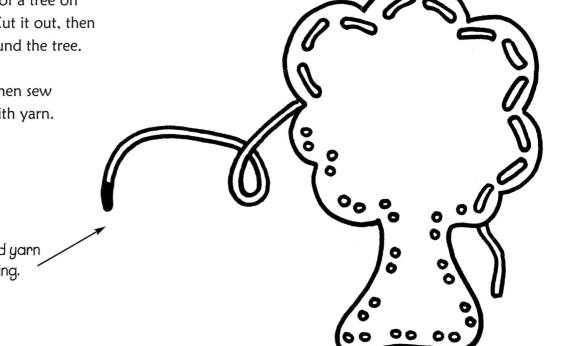

Wrap tape around yarn end for easy sewing.

Finished Sewing
Card Tree

MORE BIG FUN!

★ Plant a lemon, orange, or grapefruit seed and watch it grow.

★ Take a nature walk. Learn the name of a tree.

★ Draw a picture of the same tree in winter, spring, summer, and fall.

★ Take some paper and crayons outdoors and do bark rubbings. Does the bark feel *smooth*? *Bumpy*? *Rough*?

★ Look at the leaves on different trees. How do they look *alike*? How are they *different* from each other?

Sawdust Bugs

When you go out for a walk,
Please take a look around;
You'll see creatures in the air
And crawling on the ground.

Here's What You Need

- **2 cups (500 ml) sawdust**
- **1 cup (250 ml) dry wallpaper paste**
- **Bowl**
- **Water**
- **Pipe cleaner**

Here's What You Do

1 Mix the sawdust and dry wallpaper paste in the bowl. Slowly add water until a thick dough forms.

2 Shape the dough into sawdust bugs, then poke pieces of pipe cleaner into the heads for antennae. What will you name your bugs?

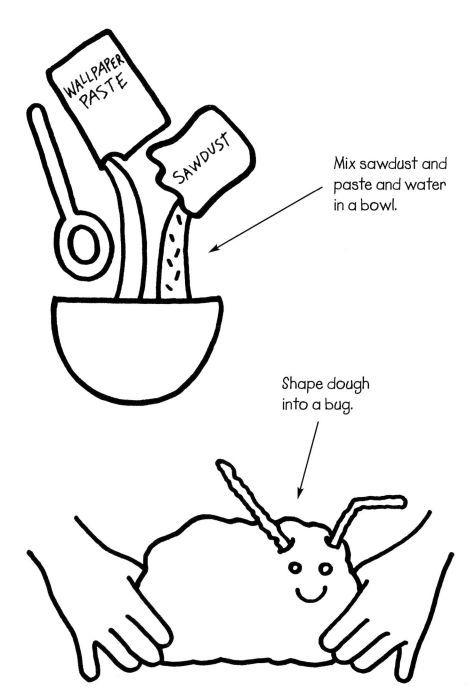

Mix sawdust and paste and water in a bowl.

Shape dough into a bug.

Paint when dough is dry.

Finished
Sawdust Bug

MORE BIG FUN!

★ Make a whole bug collection—*big* ones, *little* ones, *long* ones, *short* ones, *fat* ones, *thin* ones, *scary* ones, and *silly* ones.

★ Collect leaves, twigs, acorns, and other natural materials to glue onto cardboard to make a nature collage.

★ Place leaves from different trees under thin sheets of paper, then rub a crayon over the tops for leaf rubbings. Staple the sheets together to make a book about trees.

Fantastic Footprints

If you ride a dinosaur,
Hold onto its long neck—
And slow it down by shouting,
"Whoa, Tyrannosaurus Rex!"

Pour paint into one tray.

Here's What You Need

- **Newspaper**
- **Poster paint**
- **2 Styrofoam trays (from fruits or vegetables)**
- **Child safety scissors**
- **Large sheet of paper**

Cut foot shape from second tray.

Here's What You Do

1 Cover table with newspaper. Pour a small amount of paint into one Styrofoam tray.

2 Cut the shape of a dinosaur foot from the other tray, then dip into the paint and press down onto the paper for dinosaur footprints.

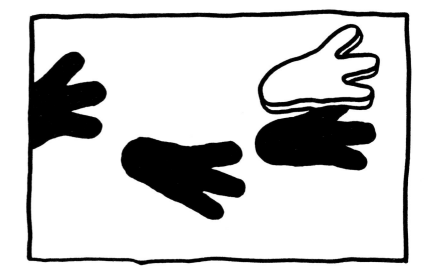

Dip foot shape into paint, and press onto paper.

Finished Fantastic
Footprints

MORE BIG FUN!

★ Be a print detective! Look for footprints and paw prints in the sand or snow. Can you guess *who* made them? Can you tell from *where* they were coming and where they were going?

★ Dip your feet in water and leave footprints behind on the pavement.

★ Make paw prints on steamy windows or mirrors by pressing your palm and just the tips of your fingers to the glass.

Sock Puppet Pet

Parakeets, a cockatoo,
A turtle, fish, or frog—
There are lots of pets to love
Besides a cat or dog!

Here's What You Need

- **2 old socks**
- **Child safety scissors**
- **3 rubber bands**
- **Scrap fabric**
- **White craft glue**

Here's What You Do

1 Stuff one sock into the other (do not go as far as the toe).

2 Cut the toe down the center and wind a rubber band around each half of the sock's toe for ears. Wrap another rubber band around the bottom of the stuffing for a neck.

5 Cut a hole on both sides of the sock for your fingers to become the arms.

4 Cut out fabric scraps for the puppet's eyes, mouth, and nose; then glue them onto your puppet pet.

Cut down center for ears.

Stuff one sock into the other.

Cut out arm hole.

Cut out arm hole.

Finished Sock
Puppet Pet

MORE BIG FUN!

★ Make several sock puppet pets and have a puppet show.

★ Cut pictures of animals from old magazines in half. Invent new animals by putting unmatched halves together.

★ Read *Socks for Supper* by Jack Kent.

★ Name your sock puppet pets. What's a good name for a sock bunny?

ARGYLE

Four Season Trees

When autumn leaves fall from the trees,
They flutter to the ground.
Rake them all up and you will find
There's always more around.

Here's What You Need

- **2 toilet tissue tubes**
- **Child safety scissors**
- **4 pieces of shirt cardboard**
- **White craft glue**
- **Poster paint (assorted colors including brown)**
- **Paintbrush**

Here's What You Do

1 Hold the tubes upright, then ask a grownup to cut them in half vertically (up and down). Glue each half onto one piece of shirt cardboard for tree trunks. Let dry completely.

2 Paint the tube tree trunks brown. Paint branches and seasonal leaves on the cardboard, or collect leaves outdoors to glue on.

Cut tubes in half vertically.

Draw branches.

Glue tube halves onto cardboard.

Draw or glue on leaves.

Finished Four Season Tree

MORE BIG FUN!

★ Press autumn leaves between clear contact paper, then punch a hole in the top and hang from a string.

School Days

Noodle Nametag

When the school year starts,
Summer draws to an end.
It's a great time
To make new friends!

Here's What You Need

- **Shirt cardboard**
- **Child safety scissors**
- **Poster paint**
- **Paintbrush**
- **Tape**
- **Large safety pin**
- **Alphabet noodles**
- **White craft glue**

Cut rectangle out of cardboard.

|← 4" →|
1"

Here's What You Do

1 Cut the cardboard into a 4" x 1" (10 cm x 2.5 cm) rectangle. Paint it with the poster paint. It can be a solid color or any design you like. Let dry completely.

Tape safety pin to back.

2 Ask a grownup to help you tape the safety pin to the back.

3 Use the alphabet noodles to spell your name. Glue them onto the front of the cardboard. Let dry completely. Then, if you want, you can paint the noodles.

Glue noodles on front to spell your name.

A • B • C

Finished Noodle
Nametag

MORE BIG FUN!

★ Use other pasta shapes to spell a name or message on a larger piece of cardboard, then hang it with string around a doorknob.

★ Read *Annabelle Swift, Kindergartner* by Amy Schwartz.

★ Ask a partner to draw letters (with a finger) on the palm of your hand while you close your eyes. Can you guess what the letters are? Take turns drawing and guessing.

A · B · C

Teachers make a classroom
An exciting place to learn.
"Call on me! I know the answer!"
Each student shouts in turn.

Here's What You Need

- **Newspaper**
- **Apple**
- **Paper towel**
- **Fabric paint**
- **Heavy paper plate**
- **Plain canvas tote bag or brown bag with handle (see page 106)**

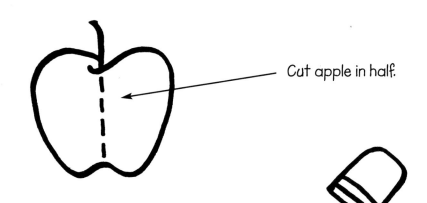

Cut apple in half.

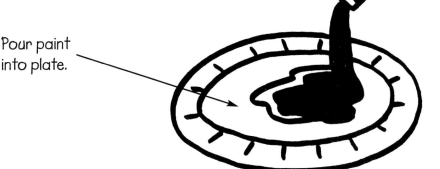

Pour paint into plate.

Here's What You Do

1 Cover the table with newspaper. Ask a grownup to use a knife to cut the apple in half. Pat dry the cut side of the apple with the paper towel.

2 Pour a thin layer of fabric paint into the plate. Dip the flat side of the apple into the paint. Press onto the bag for apple prints. Let dry completely.

Dip flat side of apple into paint, then press down on bag.

A • B • C

Finished Apple
Print Book Bag

MORE BIG FUN!

★ Use poster paint to print apples on brown paper bags, then wrap your books with the printed paper.

★ Try printing with vegetables, such as carrots, celery, onions, and potatoes.

★ Talk about your favorite books. What makes them special to you?

★ Make prints on old pillowcases or undershirts.

Sandpaper Letter Rubbings

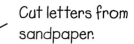

The alphabet's many letters
Begin with ABC;
They spell big words like
    "atmosphere"
And little ones like "be"!

Here's What You Need

- **Sheet of sandpaper**
- **Child safety scissors**
- **White craft glue**
- **Cardboard**
- **Thin white paper**
- **Crayons**

Here's What You Do

1   Cut letters from the sandpaper, then glue letters onto cardboard. Let dry completely.

2   Lay thin paper over the sandpaper. Rub crayons back and forth until letters appear.

Cut letters from sandpaper.

Lay thin paper over cardboard.

Glue letters on cardboard.

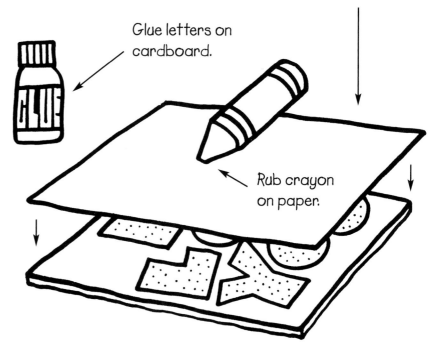

Rub crayon on paper.

A • B • C

Finished Sandpaper Letter Rubbing

MORE BIG FUN!

★ Write your initials with sandpaper letters.

A.T.I.

★ Read *Chicka Chicka Boom Boom* by Bill Martin.

★ Close your eyes and feel the sandpaper. Can you guess what letter it is?

Color Match Game

Red spaghetti, purple peas,
And bright-green cookie dough—
If colors are all mixed up,
You'll have a food rainbow!

Color one side of two
cards the same color.

Here's What You Need

- **Crayons**
- **Index cards**

Here's What You Do

1 Use each crayon to color one side of two index cards. If you want, you can also write the name of the color on the cards.

Mix up cards, color-side down.

2 Place cards color-side down, and mix them up. To play the game, turn cards over two at a time until a match is made. Continue until all colors are matched.

3 Play with a friend. (You lose a turn if there is no match.)

A · B · C

Finished Color Match Game

MORE BIG FUN!

⭐ Draw two pictures or shapes that are the same color on two index cards. Turn cards over, and play the matching game.

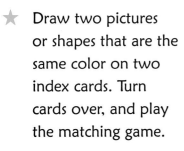

⭐ Make colored ice cubes by adding food coloring to the water

before freezing. Watch two different colors melt together in a glass.

⭐ Are your favorite foods all one color, or do you like a "rainbow" of foods?

🌂 · A · ☁ · B · ☀ · C · ⛈

Sparkling Shapes Mobile

A shape that's neither square nor round
Has a funny name:
It's called an octagon and has
Eight sides all the same!

Here's What You Need

- **Glitter**
- **Clear contact paper**
- **Child safety scissors**
- **Hole punch**
- **String**
- **Wire hanger**
- **Tape**

Here's What You Do

1 Sprinkle glitter onto sticky side of contact paper. Cover with a second piece of contact paper. Cut the contact paper into shapes.

2 Punch a hole in the top of each shape, then thread different lengths of string through each hole.

3 Tie sparkling shapes to the wire hanger with string. Tape to hold in place.

Glitter

Sticky side

Cover with other sheet of contact paper, sticky-sides together.

Cut out shapes.

Punch hole and thread with string.

A · B · C

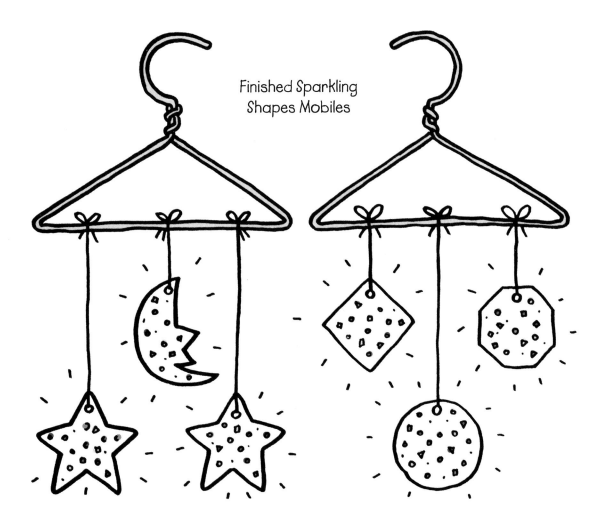

Finished Sparkling
Shapes Mobiles

MORE BIG FUN!

★ Sprinkle hole-punch-paper circles or confetti onto contact paper; then cut into shapes, and tie to a wire hanger to make a mobile.

★ Go on a shape hunt around your home or school.

How many *circles* can you find. *Squares? Triangles?*

★ Think of some things that sparkle. Look at different kinds of rocks, the stars in the sky, or the surface of the water on a sunny day.

☂ · A · ☁ · B · ☀ · C · ⛈

Cereal Counter

It's easy to count toes
And the slices in a pie—
Much harder to count stars
Glowing brightly in the sky!

Here's What You Need

- **Beverage stir stick or thin drinking straw**
- **Play dough**
- **Cheerios**

Here's What You Do

1 Stand stir stick or straw upright in play dough.

2 Count each Cheerio as it slides down the stick.

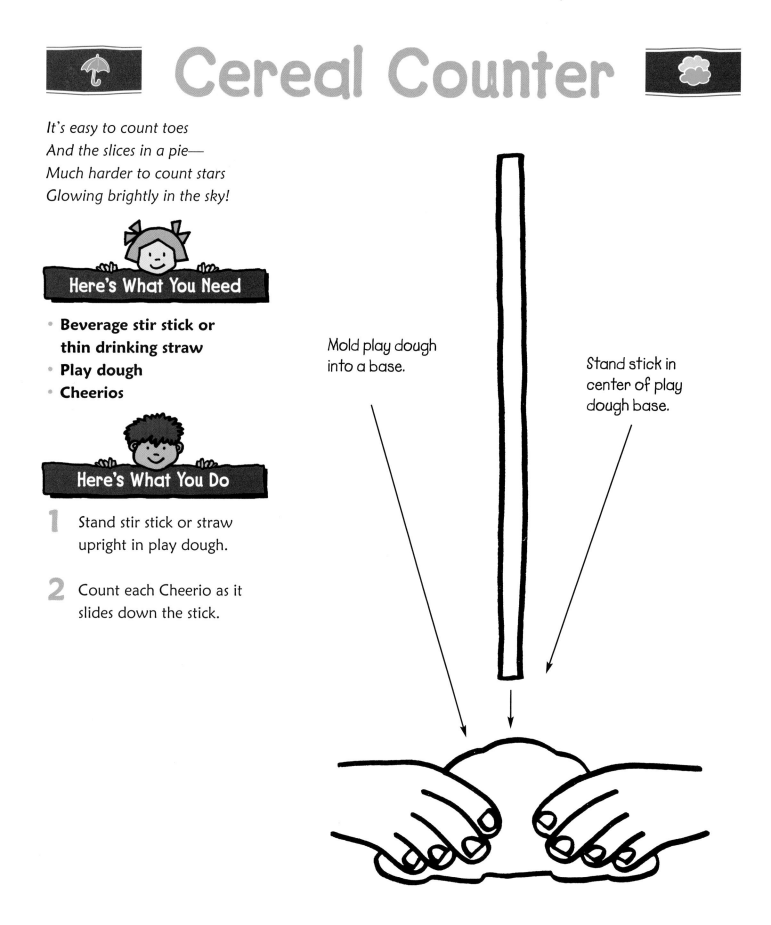

Mold play dough into a base.

Stand stick in center of play dough base.

A · B · C

Finished Cereal
Counter

MORE BIG FUN!

★ Use an egg carton, muffin tin, or plastic tub to sort things such as pasta, beans, acorns, or seashells.

★ Count how many blocks you can stack before they topple over.

★ How many red cars do you see when riding in the car?

★ Chant the poem, "One, Two, Buckle My Shoe!"

A • B • C

Cookie Sheet Clock

Clocks tick away the seconds,
Count minutes in the day;
They tell you when it's bedtime
And when it's time to play.

Cut circles and clock hands from Styrofoam.

Here's What You Need

- **Styrofoam trays (from fruits or vegetables)**
- **Child safety scissors**
- **Magnetic tape**
- **Marker**
- **Cookie sheet**

Here's What You Do

1 Cut twelve circles and the hands of a clock from Styrofoam trays.

2 Attach a small strip of magnetic tape to the back of each circle and the clock's hands.

3 Write the numbers 1 through 12 on the circles, then place them onto the cookie sheet to make a clock. Point the clock's hands to tell time.

Attach magnetic tape strips on back of circles and hands.

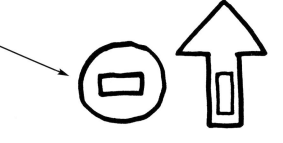

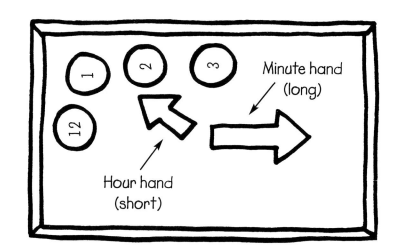

Minute hand (long)

Hour hand (short)

Finished Cookie
Sheet Clock

MORE BIG FUN!

★ Move the hands
of the clock to tell
what time you go
to bed. Then read
Bedtime for Frances
by Russell Hoban.

★ *Count* how many clocks
are in your house. How
many have digital (print-
out) numbers? How
many have hands?

★ Draw a picture of your
favorite time of day.

Weather Watch Board

When it's sunny in the morning,
And then the sky turns gray,
It's time to put your slicker on,
'Cause rain is on the way!

Here's What You Need

- **Large shoebox**
- **Markers**
- **Felt (assorted colors)**
- **Child safety scissors**
- **White craft glue**
- **Sticky-backed Velcro**

Here's What You Do

1 Trace the shoe-box lid onto a large felt scrap, then cut out felt and glue to the top of the lid.

2 Draw weather shapes such as a sun, clouds, an umbrella, and a snowman onto the remaining felt. Cut out the shapes, and decorate with markers. Attach Velcro to their backs.

3 Look for signs that hint what the weather will be tomorrow. Place your prediction shape on the Weather Watch Board before you go to bed. The next morning, check to see if you were right.

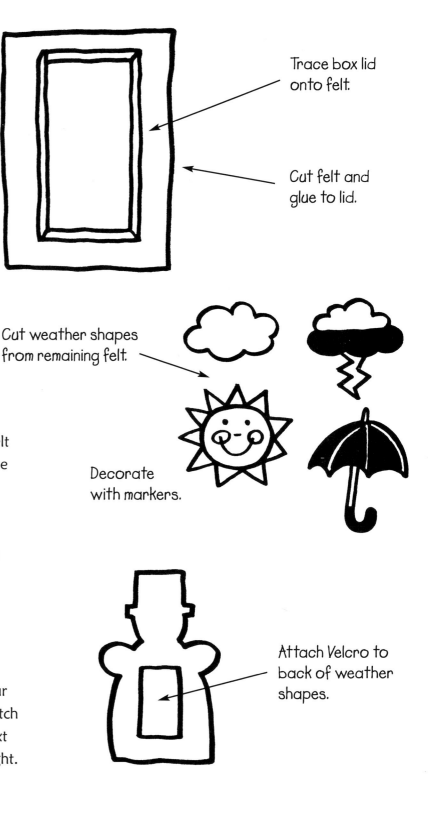

Trace box lid onto felt.

Cut felt and glue to lid.

Cut weather shapes from remaining felt.

Decorate with markers.

Attach Velcro to back of weather shapes.

Finished Weather
Watch Board

★ Use puffy fabric paint to decorate the felt shapes.

★ There are many signs that help us predict what is about to happen. Can you tell when a thunderstorm is near? Are the clouds heavy and dark? Is the dog hiding?

What are the signs of a snowstorm? A very hot day?

★ Draw lines every ½" (1 cm) up the side of a clear plastic cup, then place outside and wait for rain. *How much* rain fell during the storm?

Polka-Dot Lunch Bag

Try packing lunch that's tasty
And also good for you;
Make sandwiches on
  whole-grain bread—
Add fruits and veggies too!

Here's What You Need

- **Newspaper**
- **Poster paint**
- **Heavy paper plate**
- **Pencil (with eraser)**
- **Small brown paper bag**

Here's What You Do

1 Cover the table with newspaper. Pour a thin layer of paint into a heavy paper plate.

2 Dip the eraser into the paint, then press onto the bag for polka-dots. Let dry completely before packing lunch.

Finished
Polka-Dot
Lunch Bag

MORE BIG FUN!

★ Use the eraser to print a name or special message on the lunch bag.

★ Play connect-the-dots on the bag when you're done with lunch.

★ Talk about your favorite foods for lunch. How do they taste? Are they *salty* like pretzels? *Sweet* like sugar? *Sour* like pickles?

A • B • C

Big Fun Crafts

Bottle Bowling Pins

The bowling ball is headed
Straight toward the pins;
And if every pin falls down,
You're the one who wins!

Here's What You Need

- **Large plastic soda bottles**
- **Funnel**
- **Clean sand**
- **Stickers**
- **Tennis ball**

Here's What You Do

1 Rinse out bottles and soak in warm water to remove the labels. Let dry completely.

2 Use the funnel to fill the bottles one-third full of sand. Screw tops back on bottles.

3 Decorate bottles with stickers.

4 Arrange bottles (at least three) for a bowling game. How many pins can you knock down with one ball?

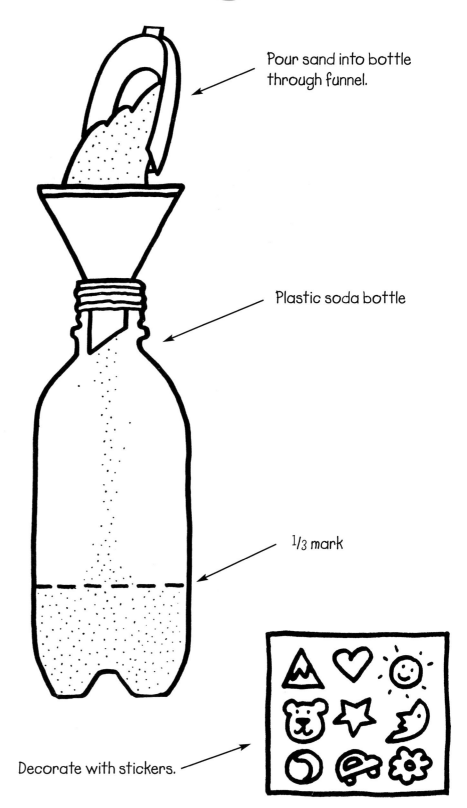

Pour sand into bottle through funnel.

Plastic soda bottle

1/3 mark

Decorate with stickers.

Finished Bottle Bowling Pins

MORE BIG FUN!

★ Visit a bowling alley. *Listen* to the sounds of the rolling balls and falling pins.

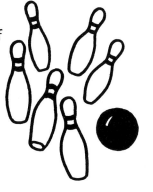

★ Can you pick up a bowling ball? It is very *heavy*. Maybe you can ask to *touch* a ball, to *feel* the chalk dust, and *rub* your hand on the smooth bowling alley floor. Then have fun watching someone bowl.

Bobbing Boat

A boat bobs on the ocean,
And wind fills up the sail.
It could be a rough ride,
So hold onto the rail!

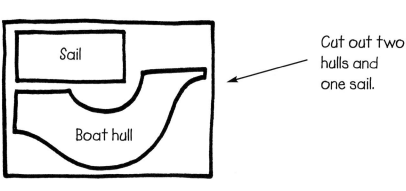

Cut out two hulls and one sail.

Here's What You Need

- **Shirt cardboard**
- **Child safety scissors**
- **Markers**
- **Scrap fabric**
- **White craft glue**
- **Popsicle stick**
- **Hole punch**
- **Thread**

Here's What You Do

1 Cut the shape of two hulls and one sail from shirt cardboard. Decorate the hull with markers.

2 Trace the cardboard sail twice onto scrap fabric. Cut out and glue fabric on both sides of the cardboard sail.

3 Press Popsicle stick between two hulls, then glue together. Glue sail onto Popsicle stick. Let dry completely.

4 Punch a hole in top of the sail, and hang boat with thread.

Cut out two sails from fabric. Glue onto cardboard sail.

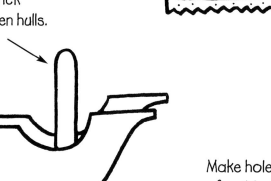

Glue stick between hulls.

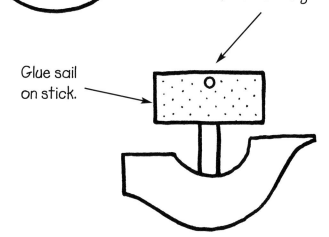

Make hole in top of sail to hang.

Glue sail on stick.

Finished
Bobbing Boat

MORE BIG FUN!

★ Make a boat mobile. Make several boats, and hang them from a branch or wire coat hanger.

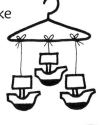

★ Glue your boat onto paper and paint the ocean and sky.

★ Sing the song, "Sailing, Sailing, Over the Ocean Blue."

★ Cut out pictures in magazines of different kinds of boats. Have you ever been on a ferry? A sailboat? A fishing boat? A canoe?

Pie Tin Wind Chime

Wind fills the sails on boats
And whistles through the trees;
Kites fly high in the sky,
And chimes ring in the breeze!

Poke holes around rim and center of pie tin.

Here's What You Need

• **Pie tin**
• **Pointed tool (for grownup use only)**
• **String or yarn**
• **Child safety scissors**
• **Metal spoons**

Here's What You Do

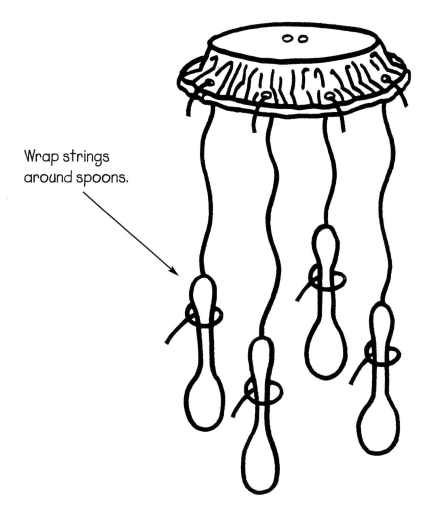

Wrap strings around spoons.

1 Turn pie tin upside down. Ask a grownup to use the pointed tool to poke holes around the rim and in the center of the tin.

2 Cut string or yarn into different lengths (save a long piece to hang the finished wind chime up). Tie string through holes.

3 Wrap string around spoons, and hang in an open window or outside.

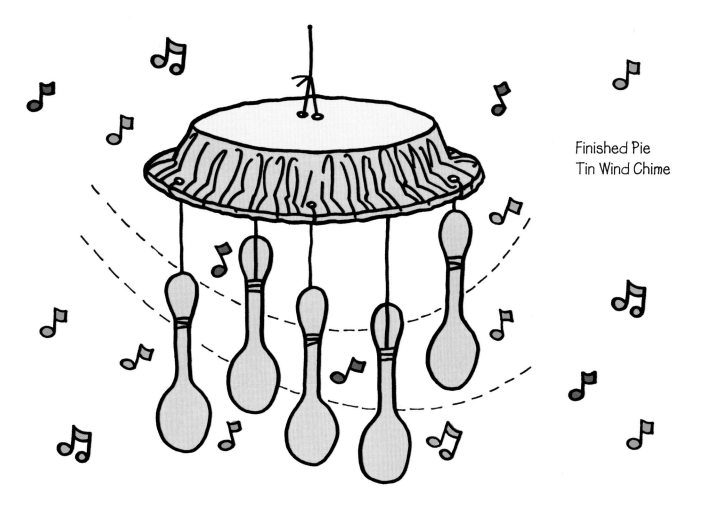

Finished Pie
Tin Wind Chime

MORE BIG FUN!

★ String seashells, nails, aluminum-can flip-tops, or bottle caps from a pie tin to make a wind chime.

★ Staple together a sheet of construction paper to form a long tube. Poke two holes in top edge and tie a string through to hang, then glue long streamers at the bottom to make a windsock.

★ Listen to the sound the wind makes on a windy day. Do the trees' leaves *rustle*? Are flags *waving*? What other signs tell you the wind is blowing?

Cardboard Carton Storage Cart

Place your books back on the shelf;
Put all your toys away.
Make your bed, pick up your clothes—
It must be clean-up day!

Here's What You Need

- **Cardboard box**
- **Child safety scissors**
- **Shirt cardboard**
- **Wrapping paper**
- **Tape**
- **Markers**
- **White craft glue**
- **Paper fasteners**

Here's What You Do

1 Cut four 1" (2.5 cm) squares from the lid of the cardboard box. Cut four wheels from shirt cardboard. Decorate wheels with markers, and poke a hole through the center of wheels and squares.

2 Wrap box in paper and tape in place. Glue squares on the outside of the box where the wheels are to be mounted. Use a fastener to attach decorative wheels on the sides of the box.

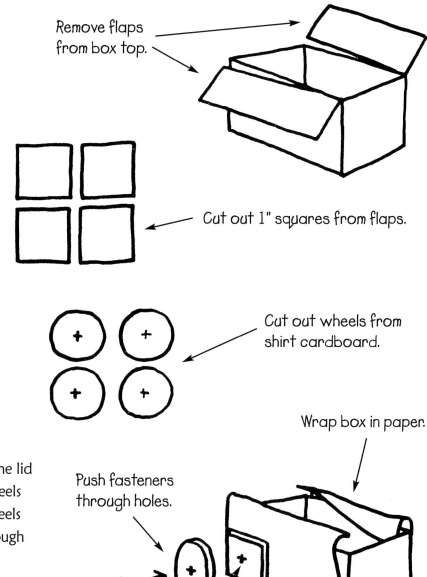

Remove flaps from box top.

Cut out 1" squares from flaps.

Cut out wheels from shirt cardboard.

Wrap box in paper.

Push fasteners through holes.

Poke holes.

Glue squares on box.

Finished Cardboard
Carton Storage Box

MORE BIG FUN!

★ Store toys, clothes, puzzle pieces, or games in your cart.

★ Play a beat-the-clock game: use an egg timer or stopwatch and see how many minutes it takes to clean up your room. Next time, try to do it faster.

★ Put on your favorite music when doing chores. You can work to the beat and hum along too.

Picture Puzzle

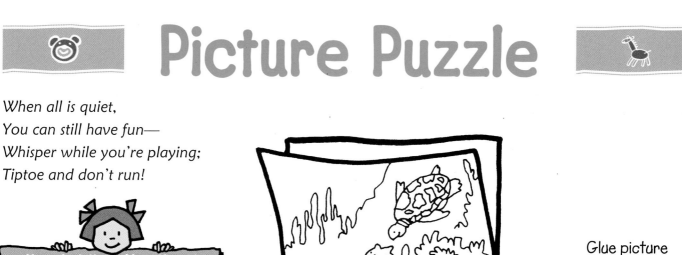

When all is quiet,
You can still have fun—
Whisper while you're playing;
Tiptoe and don't run!

Here's What You Need

- **Old magazines**
- **Child safety scissors**
- **Cardboard**
- **White craft glue**
- **Markers**

Here's What You Do

1 Cut out a picture from an old magazine. Glue it onto cardboard, and trim the edges. Let dry completely.

2 On the back of the cardboard, draw puzzle pieces. Cut out along the lines.

3 Put pieces together to make a puzzle. The smaller the pieces, the more difficult the puzzle.

Glue picture on cardboard.

Draw puzzle pieces on back of cardboard, and cut along lines.

Finished
Picture Puzzle

MORE BIG FUN!

★ Glue a drawing or large photograph onto cardboard, then cut out the pieces to make a puzzle.

★ Play card games, read a book, draw a picture, or put photos in an album during "please-be-quiet" times.

★ Sometimes when people are confused, they are said to be *puzzled*. Have you ever been *puzzled* about something?

Cardboard Box Bookshelves

When you have a question,
The answer's in a book.
Librarians can help
By showing where to look!

Here's What You Need

- **Newspaper**
- **Poster paint**
- **Paper plate**
- **Paintbrush**
- **3 cardboard boxes—each approx. 10" x 13" x 9" (25 cm x 32.5 cm x 22.5 cm)**

Here's What You Do

1 Cover table with newspaper, then pour a small amount of paint into the plate. Paint boxes with poster paint. Let dry completely.

2 Stack boxes or place them side-by-side for bookshelves.

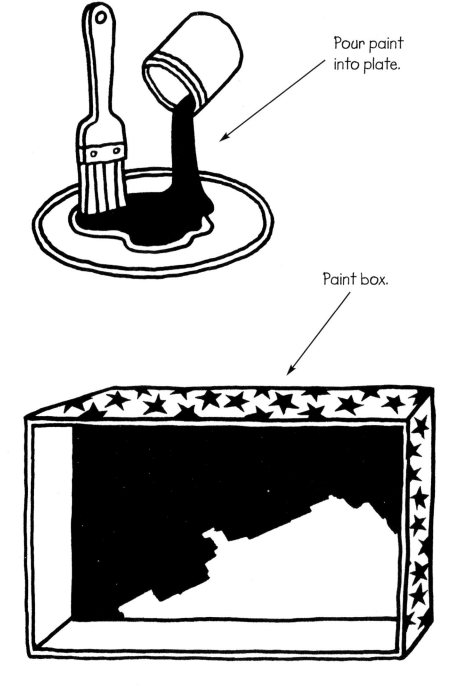

Pour paint into plate.

Paint box.

Finished Cardboard Box Bookshelves

MORE BIG FUN!

★ Decorate the bookshelf boxes with stickers or sponge paint (see page 96).

★ Visit your library and apply for a library card.

★ Find out if your library has a story hour. A librarian will read many wonderful books to you and your friends.

★ Sort your books by *kinds* (mysteries, science, stories) or by *author*. Stack them together in your bookcase.

Tray Sailboat

Create a boat from paper;
Try making two or three.
Set sail upon the water—
Pretend you've gone to sea!

Here's What You Need

- **Styrofoam tray (from fruits or vegetables)**
- **Child safety scissors**
- **Toothpick**
- **Construction paper**
- **Markers**
- **Stapler**
- **Straw**

Here's What You Do

1 Cut the shape of a boat from the Styrofoam tray. Poke the toothpick into the Styrofoam.

2 Cut a sail from construction paper, and decorate.

3 Staple the sail onto the straw and slip the straw over the toothpick.

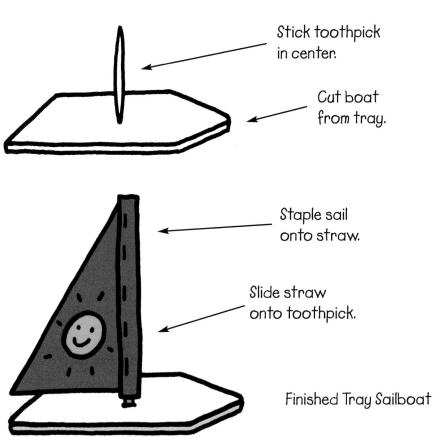

Stick toothpick in center.

Cut boat from tray.

Staple sail onto straw.

Slide straw onto toothpick.

Finished Tray Sailboat

MORE BIG FUN!

★ For a sailing painting, dampen white paper with water. Brush on poster paint for sea and sky. Let dry. Use markers to draw boats on the water.

★ What kind of boats go the *fastest*? The *slowest*? Which kind would you use on a *pond*? On a *lake*? On the *ocean*?

Family Fun

"All About Me" Scrapbook

It's fun to have a scrapbook
Of your very own
For looking at the pictures
To see just how you've grown!

Here's What You Need

- **Construction paper**
- **White paper**
- **White craft glue**
- **Hole punch**
- **Ribbon or ring binders**
- **Markers**
- **Old family photos**

Here's What You Do

1 Glue white paper onto the sheets of construction paper for the book's pages.

2 Punch three holes down the side of each sheet (be sure to put the holes in the same place on each page), then put ribbon or ring binders through the holes to hold the pages together.

3 Draw with markers, or glue on old photos to make a book all about you.

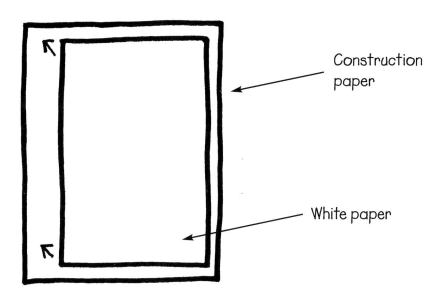

Construction paper

White paper

Use a hole punch to make three holes in each sheet.

Finished "All About Me" Scrapbook

★ Talk to grandparents or other friends about how times have changed since they were children. What kind of transportation did they have? What was the *same*? What was *different*?

★ Keep a growth chart on your bedroom wall. Ask a grownup to mark how tall you are on each birthday.

Handprint Family Tree

It's hard to think of grandparents
As kids like you or me,
Who once enjoyed a game of tag
and climbing up a tree!

Here's What You Need

- **Styrofoam tray (from fruits or vegetables)**
- **Poster paint (brown)**
- **Paint roller**
- **Roll of shelf paper or butcher paper**
- **Construction paper**
- **Marker**
- **Child safety scissors**
- **White craft glue**

Here's What You Do

Roll paint onto paper
in the shape of a tree.

FAMILY TREE

1 Pour a thin layer of paint into the tray, then roll paint onto the paper to make a tree trunk and enough branches for each person in your family. Let dry completely.

2 Trace hands onto construction paper, then cut them out.

Glue cut-out
paper hands
onto tree.

3 Glue paper hands onto tree branches. Write names and birthdates on each paper hand.

Finished Handprint
Family Tree

★ Press hands in puffy fabric paint, then onto a T-shirt. Use a fabric marker to write names and birthdates.

★ Draw a portrait of your grand-parents; then frame it with Popsicle sticks, and give it as a gift.

★ Talk about the ways people change as they grow up. Look at a baby picture of yourself. Have you gotten *taller* since you were a baby? Do you have more hair? How are you *different* from a grownup?

"We're So Proud!" Medal

When someone in the family
Deserves your admiration,
Show how proud you are
With a big celebration!

Here's What You Need

- **Shirt cardboard**
- **Child safety scissors**
- **White craft glue**
- **String or yarn**
- **Recycled aluminum foil**
- **Hole punch**

Here's What You Do

1 Cut a circle from the cardboard. Squeeze glue in a design on the cardboard, then press string or yarn into the glue. Let dry completely.

2 Wrap foil around the cardboard. Use your finger to gently press around the string design.

3 Punch a hole in the top of the medal. Thread string or yarn through the hole to wear loosely around the neck.

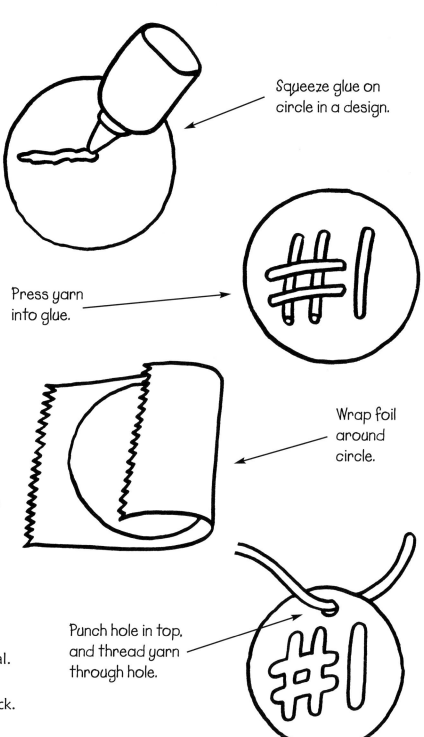

Squeeze glue on circle in a design.

Press yarn into glue.

Wrap foil around circle.

Punch hole in top, and thread yarn through hole.

Finished "We're So Proud!" Medal

MORE BIG FUN!

★ Plan a special dinner and serve the award winner's favorite food.

★ Cut a band of construction paper 18" wide (45 cm). Measure the length to fit around the head, then cut a zigzag shape into the top of the band. Overlap the ends and tape together to make an award winner's crown.

★ Talk about what it means to be proud of yourself or someone else. Whom or what are you *proud* of?

WINNER

MY REPORT CARD

Hearts & Flowers Necklace

There's no one better than a mom,
On those less-than-perfect days,
To warm you with her hugs and smiles
While kissing your tears away!

Here's What You Need

- **Small flower**
- **Clear contact paper**
- **Child safety scissors**
- **Hole punch**
- **Rigatoni pasta**
- **Yarn**

Here's What You Do

1 Press the flower between two pieces of contact paper. Cut into a heart shape, then punch a hole in the top of the heart.

2 String pasta and heart onto yarn. Tie ends together to form necklace.

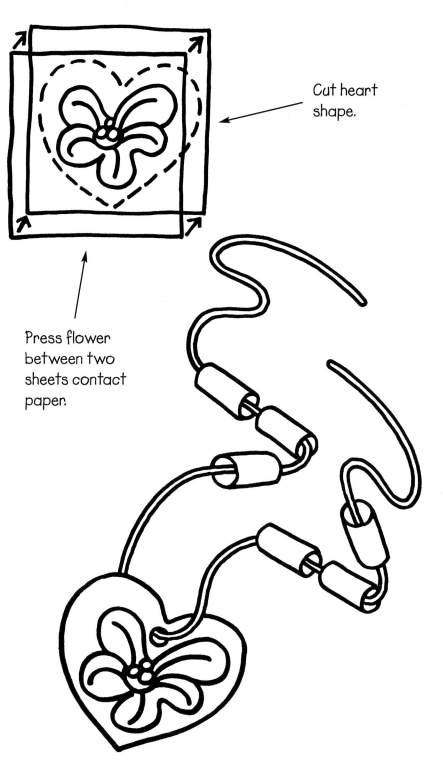

Cut heart shape.

Press flower between two sheets contact paper.

Finished Hearts &
Flowers Necklace

★ Trace handprints onto construction paper, then cut them out. Write a chore or good deed that you are willing to do on each hand. Glue the hands onto Popsicle sticks, and push them into a flowerpot to make a "helping hand" plant.

★ Learn to say "I love you" in American Sign Language.

Stocking Finger Puppet

There's something more exciting
Than TV or video:
Watch the curtain going up
On your funny puppet show!

Here's What You Need

- **Old white sock**
- **Old nylon stocking**
- **Toilet tissue tube**
- **Rubber band**
- **Scrap fabric**
- **Child safety scissors**
- **White craft glue**
- **Yarn**

Here's What You Do

1 Roll the sock into a ball, then stuff it into the toe of a nylon stocking.

2 Thread the stocking through the cardboard tube until the puppet's head (sock) rests on top. Pull excess stocking back up over the outside of the tube, and secure with a rubber band.

3 Use fabric to cover cardboard tube. Glue on scrap fabric for puppet's eyes, nose, and mouth; then glue on yarn for puppet's hair. Let dry completely.

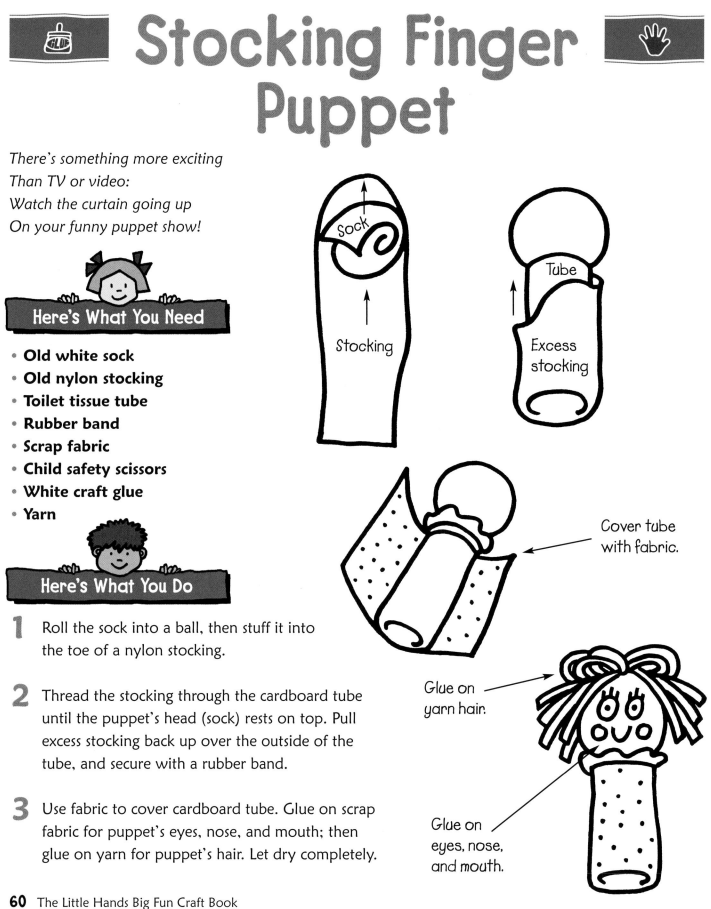

Sock

Stocking

Tube

Excess stocking

Cover tube with fabric.

Glue on yarn hair.

Glue on eyes, nose, and mouth.

Finished Stocking
Finger Puppet

MORE BIG FUN!

★ Perform a puppet show behind an old sheet hanging between two chairs.

★ Make puppets of everyone in your family. Role-play different situations at home, and try to come up with ways of solving problems.

★ Glue on cotton balls for beards, hair, and bushy eyebrows.

Cozy Kitty Pillow

Find a cozy corner,
Then turn on the light;
Pick your favorite story—
Read a book tonight!

Here's What You Need

- **Old pillowcase (solid color)**
- **Rubber bands**
- **Cardboard**
- **Fabric paint**
- **Paintbrush**
- **Round pillow form**
- **Child safety scissors**
- **Yarn (black)**
- **Fabric glue**
- **Long ribbon or yarn**

Here's What You Do

1 Wrap rubber bands around two corners of the pillowcase for kitty's ears.

2 Insert cardboard into pillowcase, then use fabric paint to paint on a kitty's face. Let dry completely.

3 Remove cardboard and insert the round pillow form. Cut short pieces of black yarn for whiskers, and glue onto kitty's face. Let dry, and tie a ribbon or yarn tightly around the bottom.

Wrap rubber bands around corners for ears.

Insert cardboard, and paint face.

Insert form, and glue on yarn whiskers.

Tie yarn or ribbon around bottom.

Finished Cozy
Kitty Pillow

MORE BIG FUN!

★ Post a chart in your reading corner to keep track of the books you've read yourself or have had read to you. Next to the chart, hang a small pouch for library cards and bookmarks.

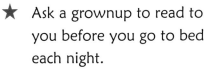

★ Invite a friend to share reading time in your cozy corner.

★ Ask a grownup to read to you before you go to bed each night.

★ Make *sound effects* to go with your favorite story: growls, thunder, screeches, or the wind.

Tooth Fairy Pouch

Don't worry if you've lost a tooth
And have a funny grin;
One day you'll be surprised to see
Another one's grown in!

Here's What You Need

- **Toilet tissue tube**
- **Stapler**
- **Scrap fabric and trim**
- **White craft glue**
- **White tissue paper**
- **Scrap of shirt cardboard**
- **Markers**
- **Tape**
- **Yarn**

Here's What You Do

1 Staple together bottom of the cardboard tube. Wrap fabric around tube and glue in place.

2 Accordion-fold tissue, and glue on back of tube for wings. Cut shape of fairy face and neck from cardboard. Draw eyes, nose, and mouth; then tape inside tube. Glue on yarn for hair.

3 Tie yarn to sides of tube and hang pouch from a doorknob or headboard. Glue on fabric trim for decoration.

Finished Tooth Fairy Pouch

MORE BIG FUN!

★ Draw a picture of what you look like when you lose a tooth.

Friendship

Friendship Paper Quilt

There was a man with a dream
Named Martin Luther King;
He wished for peace and friendship
And the love they would bring!

Here's What You Need

- **Construction paper**
- **Ruler**
- **Child safety scissors**
- **Hole punch**
- **Yarn**
- **Large needle (use only with a grownup's help)**

Here's What You Do

1 Cut construction paper into 6" x 6" (15 cm x 15 cm) squares. Punch holes around outer edges of the squares (be sure to line up holes evenly).

2 Give paper squares to friends and family. Ask each person to draw a self-portrait.

3 Ask a grownup to help you thread the needle with yarn, and sew squares together to make a Friendship Paper Quilt.

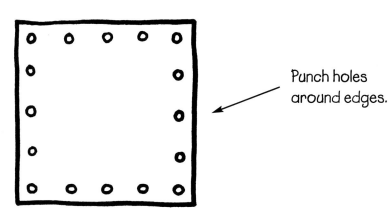

Punch holes around edges.

Collect self-portraits of family and friends.

Sew squares together.

Finished
Friendship
Paper Quilt

MORE BIG FUN!

★ Ask friends, classmates, or neighbors to write a favorite recipe on an index card. Make photocopies of the recipes, then staple together to make a friendship cookbook.

COOKBOOK

★ Are you someone's friend? What does it mean to be a friend?

★ Read *A Picture Book of Martin Luther King Jr.* by David A. Adler.

Love Plant

*Is there someone very special
To give a valentine?
Sign your name with plenty of love,
And ask, "Will you be mine?"*

Here's What You Need

- **Construction paper (red and pink)**
- **Child safety scissors**
- **Stapler**
- **Pipe cleaners**
- **Play dough or clay**
- **Small clay pot**
- **Thin strips of scrap paper**

Here's What You Do

1 Cut hearts from two sheets of construction paper. Staple the front and back of the hearts together on a pipe cleaner.

2 Place play dough in bottom of pot, then press the pipe-cleaner stems into the dough. Fill the pot with thin strips of scrap paper.

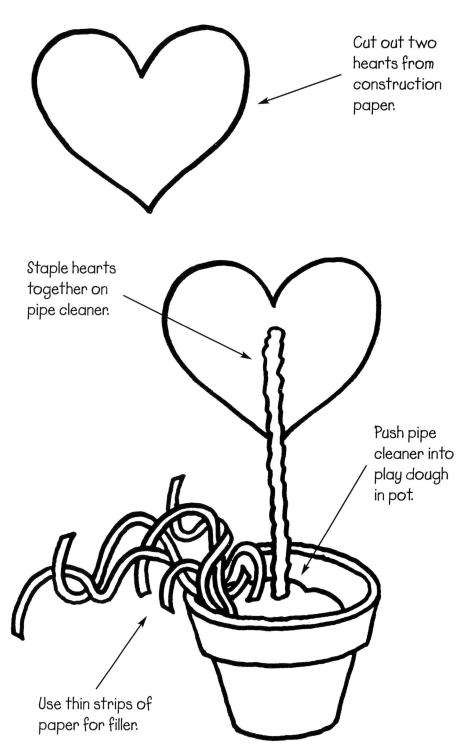

Cut out two hearts from construction paper.

Staple hearts together on pipe cleaner.

Push pipe cleaner into play dough in pot.

Use thin strips of paper for filler.

Finished Love Plant

★ Staple a cardboard heart to a paper towel tube, then paint with poster paint to make a valentine wand.

★ Do something nice for your friends, like baking brownies or helping them with chores.

★ Make a "Love the Earth" collage. Glue on pictures of things that *smell*, *feel*, and *remind* you of how special our Earth is to all of us.

Tea Party Placemat

Gather your stuffed animals
To keep you company,
And join them at the table
For a party and tea!

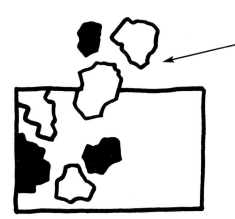

Glue torn tissue paper on construction paper.

Here's What You Need

- **Tissue paper (assorted colors)**
- **White craft glue**
- **Construction paper, 9" x 12" (22.5 cm x 30 cm)**
- **Clear contact paper**
- **Child safety scissors**

Here's What You Do

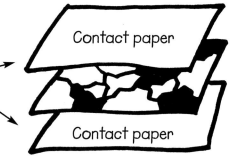

Place construction paper between sticky sides of two sheets of contact paper.

Contact paper

Contact paper

1 Tear tissue paper into small to medium-sized pieces or shapes, then glue onto construction paper.

2 Cut two sheets of clear contact paper 10" x 13" (25 cm x 32.5 cm). Place construction paper onto sticky side of one sheet, then press second sheet on top. Smooth out air bubbles and trim edges to make a placemat.

Trim edges of placemats.

3 Set a party table using the placemats, then invite your friends and their stuffed animals to tea.

Make enough for company.

Finished Tea Party Placemat

MORE BIG FUN!

★ Have a tea party with a theme. Make leaf placemats in the fall, and serve apple cider.

★ Make thin sandwiches using peanut butter, egg salad, tuna fish, or cucumbers. Use cookie cutters to cut the sandwiches into shapes.

★ Wear costumes from old clothes, hats, jewelry, and gloves. Invite an older neighbor to join you, or take the party to that person.

Friendship Bracelets

A best friend is someone
You can tell secrets to;
They laugh at all your jokes
And like being with you!

Here's What You Need

- **Paper towel tube**
- **Child safety scissors**
- **Poster paint (white)**
- **2 heavy paper plates**
- **2 small paintbrushes**
- **White craft glue**
- **Tissue paper (assorted colors)**

Here's What You Do

1 Cut two sections of cardboard tube 1½" (3.5 cm) wide for bracelets.

2 Pour a small amount of white paint into one plate. Paint bracelets with white poster paint. Let dry completely.

3 Pour a small amount of glue into the other plate, then add a few drops of water. Cut designs from tissue paper, then use paint brush to glue paper onto bracelets. Let dry completely before wearing bracelets.

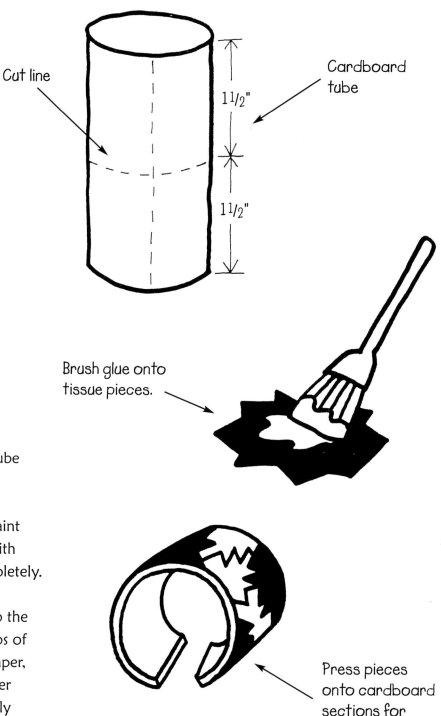

Cut line

Cardboard tube

1½"

1½"

Brush glue onto tissue pieces.

Press pieces onto cardboard sections for bracelets.

Finished
Friendship
Bracelets

MORE BIG FUN!

★ Take a picture with your friends, then glue four Popsicle sticks to fit around the photograph. Tape the photo to the back to make a framed picture.

★ Read *Frog and Toad Are Friends* by Arnold Lobel.

★ Talk about how your friends make you feel. Are you *happy* when you are with them? Do they make you laugh?

Brown Bag Turkey

Stuffed turkey in the oven,
Good friends are on the way;
Mashed potatoes, pumpkin pie . . .
Must be Thanksgiving Day!

Here's What You Need

- **Brown lunch bag**
- **Newspaper**
- **Construction paper**
- **Markers**
- **Child safety scissors**
- **Rubber band**
- **White craft glue**

Here's What You Do

1 Stuff the brown bag with sheets of crumpled newspaper. Trace a hand onto construction paper, then cut it out. Draw the head of a turkey with a long neck and waddle, then cut it out.

2 Stick the neck of the turkey into the top of the bag, then wrap a rubber band around the neck of the bag.

3 Glue the paper hand onto the bottom of the bag for turkey feathers.

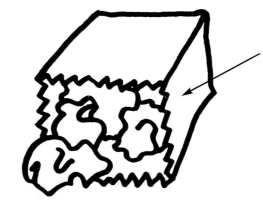

Stuff a brown bag with crumpled newspaper.

Trace a hand on construction paper.

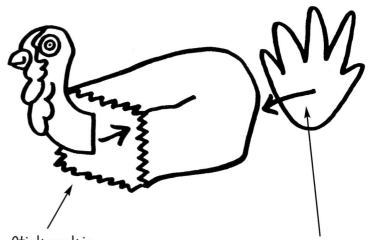

Stick neck in top of bag.

Glue hand on bottom of bag for tail feathers.

Finished Brown
Bag Turkey

MORE BIG FUN!

★ Draw Thanksgiving Day pictures on a long sheet of shelf paper. Use as a table runner when you set the holiday table.

★ Ask everyone at dinner what they are most thankful for in this past year.

★ Make a turkey puppet. Trace outstretched hand onto paper plate.

Cut out and color (the thumb is the head; other fingers are feathers). Glue onto Popsicle-stick handle

★ Cut out a large turkey from construction paper. Write a note on paper feathers about something you are thankful for. Glue them on the turkey, adding more feathers each year.

Happy Notepaper

Write a letter to some friends
Who live far away.
Tell them everything that's new,
And brighten up their day!

Finished Happy Notepaper

Here's What You Need

- **Poster paint**
- **Heavy paper plate**
- **Plastic bottle cap**
- **White stationery**
- **Markers (fine point)**

Here's What You Do

1 Pour a small amount of poster paint into the plate. Dip the bottle cap into the paint, then press onto stationery for circles. Let dry completely.

2 Draw funny faces in the circles for Happy Notepaper.

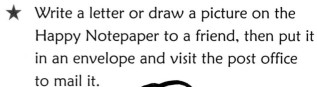

MORE BIG FUN!

★ Write a letter or draw a picture on the Happy Notepaper to a friend, then put it in an envelope and visit the post office to mail it.

S.W.A.K.

★ Use other objects to make designs on stationery, such as cookie cutters, corks, spools, thimbles, and clothespins.

Around-the-World Celebrations

America: Yankee Doodle Dandy Headband

You're invited to a party!
July fourth is a great day—
Flags will fly, and people will sing,
"Happy birthday, U.S.A.!"

Here's What You Need

- **Construction paper (red, white, and blue)**
- **Child safety scissors**
- **Stapler**
- **White craft glue**
- **Marker (red)**
- **White chalk**
- **Straws**

Here's What You Do

1 Cut a band of red, white, or blue construction paper 4" (10 cm) wide. Cut length to fit around head, then fold over and staple together to make a headband.

2 Cut white paper into four 3" x 4" (7.5 cm x 10 cm) rectangles. Cut blue paper into four 1" x 2" (2.5 cm x 5 cm) rectangles, then glue onto upper left corner of white paper for flags.

Cut a band of construction paper, fit band around head, overlap ends, and staple.

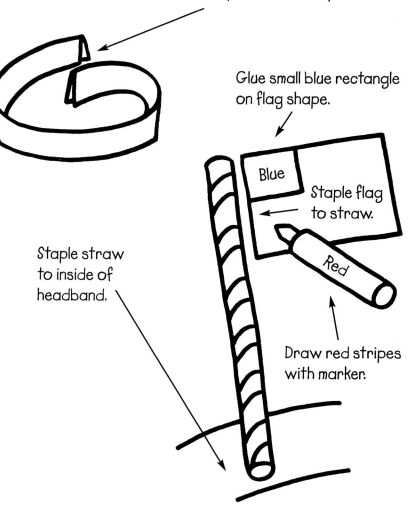

Glue small blue rectangle on flag shape.

Blue

Staple flag to straw.

Red

Staple straw to inside of headband.

Draw red stripes with marker.

3 Use the red marker to draw stripes on the flag, and the white chalk to draw on stars. Staple flags onto straws, then staple straws inside fold of headband.

Finished Yankee Doodle Dandy Headband

MORE BIG FUN!

★ Bake a Fourth of July cake. Decorate it to look like a flag with white icing, rows of strawberries for stripes and blueberries for stars.

★ March to the music of John Philip Sousa.

★ Learn to whistle "Yankee Doodle Went to Town." If you aren't a whistler, then hum it into a kazoo.

★ Talk about what it means to live in "the land of the free."

Egypt: Cracked Egg Art

Shem al Neseem *means "smell the breeze."*
Egyptians welcome spring
With roses red and fancy clothes
And families picnicking!

Here's What You Need

- **Shirt cardboard**
- **Child safety scissors**
- **Water**
- **Food coloring**
- **Cup**
- **Eggshells, washed out well**
- **Strainer**
- **Paper towels**
- **White craft glue**

Here's What You Do

1 Cut out an egg shape from the cardboard. Add water and a few drops of food coloring to a cup.

2 Break eggshells into small pieces, then place them in food coloring. Strain shells when colored. Gently dry on paper towels.

3 Cover the cardboard egg with glue, then press on egg shells.

Draw and cut out cardboard egg.

Put eggshell pieces in food coloring.

Cover egg-shaped cardboard with glue.

Apply colored shells.

Finished
Crackled
Egg Art

MORE BIG FUN!

★ Egyptians celebrate spring with a picnic breakfast. You can have a breakfast picnic too. Fill a basket with hard-boiled eggs, bread, fruit, and cheese.

★ Which other springtime holidays use eggs in the celebration? If you guessed *Easter* and *Passover*,

then you are right on track. Why do you think eggs are used in these celebrations? Where else do you see eggs in spring?

★ Find Egypt on a map or globe of the world. What continent is Egypt in? Is Egypt *close* or *far away* from where you live on the map?

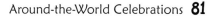

Israel: Shoebox Sukkah

The sukkah is a small hut
With branches overhead.
We celebrate the harvest
By eating fruit and bread!

Here's What You Need

- **Shoebox**
- **Child safety scissors**
- **Construction paper**
- **Markers**
- **Hole punch**
- **String**

Here's What You Do

1 Ask a grownup to help cut slits in the lid of the shoebox. Cut out one side of the box, then put the lid back on.

2 Cut construction paper into the shape of fruits and vegetables, then decorate with markers.

3 Punch hole in top of paper fruits and vegetables, and tie onto one end of string. Insert string through slit in box top and knot end of string to hold in place.

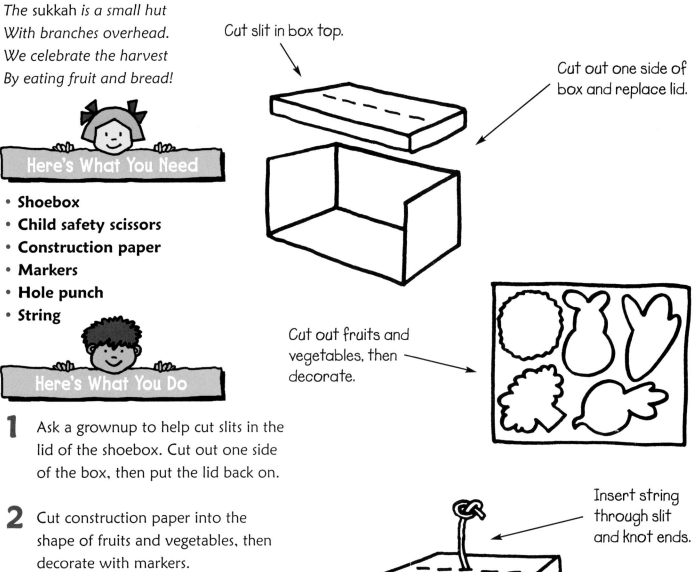

Cut slit in box top.

Cut out one side of box and replace lid.

Cut out fruits and vegetables, then decorate.

Insert string through slit and knot ends.

Attach string.

Finished
Shoebox Sukkah

MORE BIG FUN!

★ *Sukkoth* is a harvest celebration. Make a fruit or vegetable salad to celebrate your harvest season.

★ A *sukkah* is an outdoor hut, open to the sky, built to enjoy the harvest. With a grownup's help, use a needle and thread to string popcorn; then hang it from the open roof of your sukkah.

★ Ask a grownup to help you bake a *Challah*. It is the sweetened, braided bread eaten on the Jewish Sabbath and special holidays like Sukkoth.

★ Practice braiding with three pieces of heavy yarn. Once you get the method, you'll be ready to make a Challah.

Japan: Stuffed Paper Fish

In Japan on Children's Day,
Family banners fly
Along with streamers shaped like fish
From bamboo poles up high!

Here's What You Need

- **2 sheets of tissue paper**
- **Child safety scissors**
- **White craft glue**
- **Markers**
- **Used computer paper**

Here's What You Do

1 Cut a wide-mouthed fish from 2 sheets of tissue paper.

2 Squeeze a thin line of glue around the fish (leave the mouth unglued). Press the 2 sheets of tissue paper together.

3 Draw on fish's scales and eyes. Stuff the fish with torn computer paper, and glue the mouth closed.

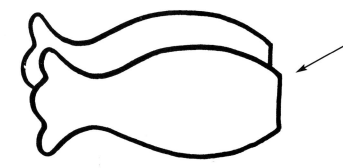

Cut out 2 fish.

Glue fish together along outer edges (not mouth).

Draw eyes, scales, and other details.

Stuff fish with torn paper.

Glue mouth closed.

Finished Stuffed Paper Fish

MORE BIG FUN!

★ Glue a pipe cleaner around the inside of the fish's mouth. Tie a long string through the fish to make a kite.

★ Japanese children display their dolls for everyone to admire on Children's Day. Dress up your dolls or stuffed animals, and show them to your friends.

★ Would you like to celebrate Children's Day where you live? Are there any special family days that seem like they are planned for children?

China: Paper Bag Dragon

Paper dragons lead the way,
The Chinese New Year has come.
Gung Hay Fat Choy means "Good luck
And happiness, everyone!"

Here's What You Need

- **Newspaper**
- **Large brown paper bag**
- **Child safety scissors**
- **Tissue paper**
- **White craft glue**
- **Poster paint**
- **Paintbrush**

Here's What You Do

1 Cover table with newspaper. Cut the bag in half on a diagonal. Cut two nostril holes in the front of the bag. (Actually, you'll use these to see out.)

2 Glue long strips of tissue paper onto the bag for streamers, then paint on colorful designs. Let dry completely before wearing your dragon costume.

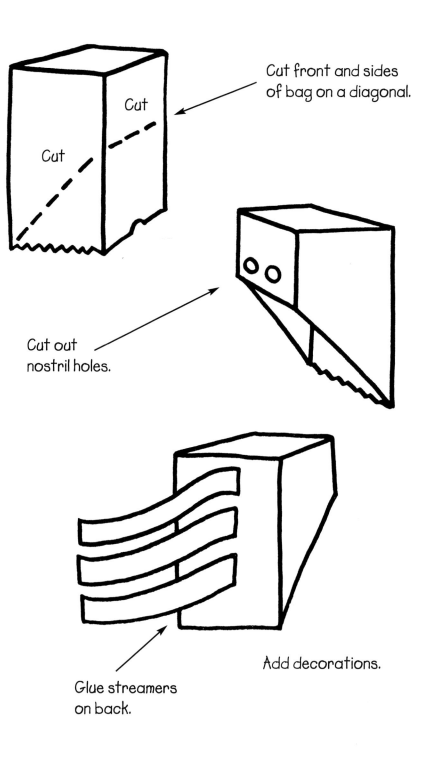

Cut front and sides of bag on a diagonal.

Cut out nostril holes.

Glue streamers on back.

Add decorations.

Finished Paper
Bag Dragon

MORE BIG FUN!

★ Red is the Chinese color for happiness and good luck. Do you have a good-luck charm or color?

★ What colors make you feel *happy*? What colors make you feel *sad*?

RED

What holidays do you celebrate that have special colors?

★ Read *Chin Chiang and the Dragon's Dance* by Ian Wallace.

Nigeria: Oatmeal Canister Drum

It's harvest in Nigeria—
Let's dance and beat tin drums!
The Zolla Festival is held
As the great New Year comes!

Here's What You Need

- **Newspaper**
- **Glossy white paper (shelf paper)**
- **Child safety scissors**
- **Large, round oatmeal canister (with top and bottom)**
- **Finger paint**
- **White craft glue**

Here's What You Do

1 Cover the table with newspaper.

2 Cut shiny white paper to fit around the container. Finger-paint designs on paper. Let dry completely.

3 Glue painted paper around canister to make a drum.

Cut white paper to fit around canister.

Paint a design on paper.

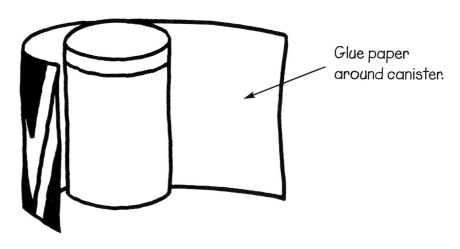

Glue paper around canister.

Finished Oatmeal
Canister Drum

MORE BIG FUN!

★ Cover a cotton ball with a square of fabric. Hold it on the end of a pencil with a rubber band to make a drumstick.

★ Ask a librarian to help you find some Nigerian or other African music. Listen to the drumbeat and play along.

★ The Nigerians are proud of their harvest. Do you do anything special to celebrate the harvest, like have a corn-on-the-cob roast or eat cucumber-and-tomato sandwiches?

★ Read *La La Salama* by Hannah Bozylinsky.

India: Flouting Diwali Candle

Far, far away in India,
Diwali *is the day*
For wearing brightly colored clothes
While candles light the way!

Here's What You Need

- **Toilet tissue tube**
- **Child safety scissors**
- **Recycled aluminum foil**
- **Construction paper scraps (red or orange)**
- **White craft glue**
- **Heavy paper bowl**

Here's What You Do

1 Cut the cardboard tube in half, then wrap it in aluminum foil.

2 Cut a flame from construction paper, and glue it to the inside of the cardboard to make a pretend candle.

3 Dip the bottom of the candle in glue, then place it in the center of the bowl. Float the bowl holding the candle in water in the sink, tub, or kiddie-pool.

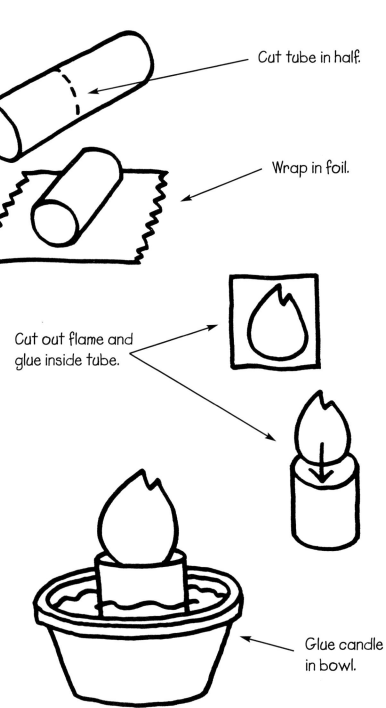

Cut tube in half.

Wrap in foil.

Cut out flame and glue inside tube.

Glue candle in bowl.

Finished Diwali Candle

MORE BIG FUN!

★ In India, candles light the way for good luck in *Diwali*, or the New Year. How do you celebrate the New Year in your home? What things do you wish for?

Jan 1

★ The walls in the homes in India are decorated with designs made with white rice-flour water and filled in with color. Mix flour and water to make a runny paste, then add a few drops of

food color. Put the mixture into squeeze bottles, and create designs on cardboard.

★ Candles are just one way people "light" their lives. Can you think of other things that make light? How about a flashlight? A lamp?

Vietnam: Swinging Lantern

Bamboo poles are strung with charms;
The smell of food is near.
Everyone is all dressed up
For Tet, Vietnamese New Year!

Here's What You Need

- **White craft glue**
- **Water**
- **Small paper bowl**
- **Tissue paper (assorted colors)**
- **Paintbrush**
- **Construction paper (white)**
- **Child safety scissors**
- **Stapler**

Here's What You Do

1 Mix glue with a few drops of water in the bowl. Tear tissue paper into small pieces, then use paintbrush to glue tissue paper onto construction paper. Let dry completely.

2 Fold construction paper in half lengthwise. Cut slits 1" (2.5 cm) apart along the fold, and stop 1" (2.5 cm) from the edge of the paper.

3 Open the paper and staple together vertically to make a lantern. Staple a strip of construction paper across the top of the lantern for a handle.

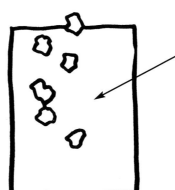

Glue tissue pieces on construction paper.

Fold paper in half, then cut 1" slits along folded side.

Open paper, staple together, then add handle.

Finished Vietnamese
Swinging Lanterns

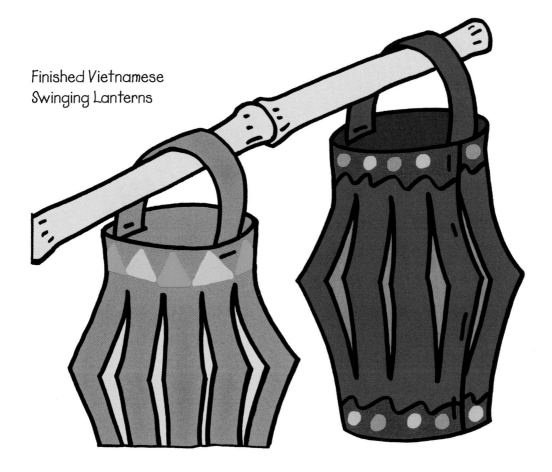

MORE BIG FUN!

★ Cut a large circle from construction paper, then make a single cut from the outside edge of the circle into the center. Overlap edges of the circle, then staple together to make a Vietnamese-style hat.

★ In Vietnam, a favorite treat for the New Year is sweetened coconut. Is there a sweet treat you eat for a special holiday?

★ The sound of firecrackers fills the air during the Vietnamese New Year. Bang a wooden spoon on the lid of a metal pot for a *loud* noise. Then tap gently for a *quiet* noise.

England: Pressed Flower Card

Fill a basket with flowers—
Today's the first of May!
Then surprise special friends
With blooms in their doorway!

Here's What You Need

- **Construction paper**
- **Child safety scissors**
- **Small flower**
- **Clear contact paper**
- **Tape**
- **Markers (assorted colors)**

Here's What You Do

1 Fold construction paper into fourths to make a greeting card. Cut out a small opening in the front fold of the card.

2 Press the flower between two pieces of contact paper, then trim to fit behind the opening in the card.

3 Tape contact paper in place. Write colorful greetings inside the card.

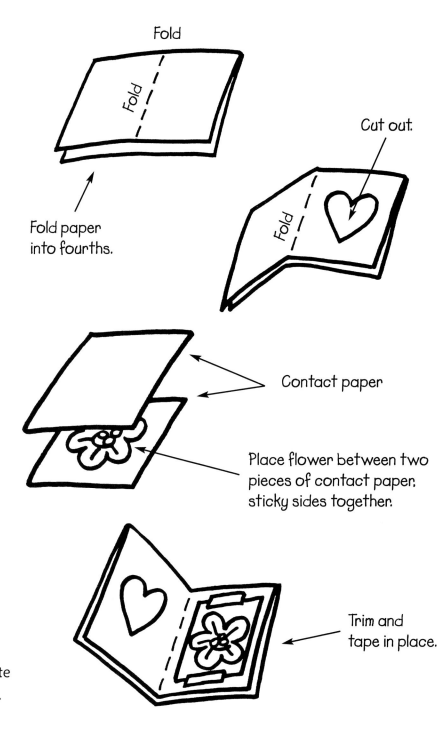

Fold

Fold

Fold paper into fourths.

Cut out.

Fold

Contact paper

Place flower between two pieces of contact paper, sticky sides together.

Trim and tape in place.

Finished Pressed
Flower Card

MORE BIG FUN!

★ Decorate a long cardboard wrapping-paper tube with brightly colored tissue-paper flowers and crepe paper streamers to make a May pole.

★ Ask permission to pick some wildflowers. How many different colors can you find? Are some colors *bright* and others *dark*?

★ It's fun to press flowers between sheets of paper towels. Put heavy books on top and allow the flowers to dry for a few days. Make a pressed-flower bouquet by gluing an arrangement of flowers on a piece of heavy paper.

Canada: Sponge Print Gift Wrap

Boxes wrapped in pretty paper—
Great gifts to give away;
Today's December 26th—
It must be Boxing Day!

Here's What You Need

- **Newspaper**
- **Sponge**
- **Child safety scissors**
- **Poster paint**
- **Heavy paper plate**
- **Roll of shelf paper**
  or butcher paper

Here's What You Do

1 Cover the table with newspaper. Cut the sponge into a shape. Pour a small amount of paint into a heavy paper plate.

2 Dip the sponge in paint, then press onto paper for prints. Let dry completely. Use paper for gift wrap.

Draw design shape on sponge, and cut out.

Dip sponge in pant, then print on paper.

Finished Sponge
Print Gift Wrap

MORE BIG FUN!

★ Print on paper with things such as bottle caps, cookie cutters, corks, and paper towel rolls.

★ Fill a long cardboard tube with small treats such as candy, toy cars, small balls, crayons, bubble bath, and a jump rope. Wrap the tube in sponge-print paper for a gift.

★ Do you think it is more fun to *give* or *receive* a gift? What's your favorite gift you ever made for someone else?

Italy: Berry Basket Cricket House

Celebrate Cricket Festival
In Florence, Italy;
Carry your crickets in a house,
And they'll chirp merrily!

Here's What You Need

- **Shirt cardboard**
- **Child safety scissors**
- **2 plastic berry baskets**
- **Lettuce leaf and grass**
- **Twist ties**

Here's What You Do

1 Cut the cardboard to fit in the bottom of one berry basket.

2 Lay cardboard, grass, and a lettuce leaf in the basket.

3 Turn the second basket upside down, and attach with twist ties for a cricket house.

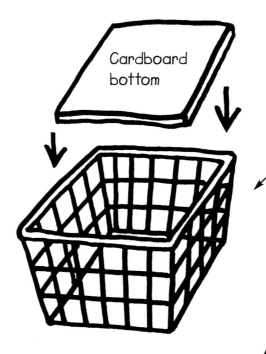

Cardboard bottom

Fit cardboard in bottom.

Attach baskets together with twist ties.

Finished Berry Basket
Cricket House

MORE BIG FUN!

★ Capture bugs in an oatmeal or cornmeal canister. Ask a grownup to cut windows in the sides of the box, then tape nylon netting inside the windows for a bug-catcher box. Always let bugs go after you look at them.

★ Read *The Very Quiet Cricket* by Eric Carle.

★ How many different things can you think of to do with berry baskets? Save them to recycle for storage and art projects.

★ Go outside on a summer's night to listen to the crickets. What other sounds do you hear?

Mexico: Seed Shaker Maraca

At a Mexican fiesta,
People celebrate all day
And gather in the evening
For a fireworks display!

Here's What You Need

- **Dried seeds (or beans)**
- **2 paper cups**
- **Masking tape**
- **Recycled aluminum foil**
- **Child safety scissors**
- **White craft glue**
- **Tissue paper (assorted colors)**

Here's What You Do

1 Place a few seeds in one cup. Turn the second cup upside down on top of the first cup. Tape cups together to make a maraca.

2 Wrap the maraca in aluminum foil, then glue on decorations cut out of tissue paper.

Put seeds in one cup.

Wrap in foil, and glue on decorations.

Tape cups together.

Finished Seed
Shaker Maracas

★ Listen to Mexican music, wear colorful clothes, and shake your maraca to the beat.

★ A *piñata* is made from papier-mâché and is filled with small toys and treats. Children in Mexico wear a blindfold as they swing a stick and try to break it open. What sweets do you eat at a festival or fair? Cotton candy? Caramel corn? Ice cream?

★ Find an old sombrero, put it on the floor, and dance around it with some friends. Ask a grownup to teach you the Mexican Hat Dance.

Around-the-World Celebrations **101**

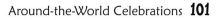

Brazil: Peek-A-Boo Carnival Mask

Come to Carnival in Brazil!
Parades are about to begin;
Everyone's singing and dancing,
So, please, do join right in!

Here's What You Need

- **Newspaper**
- **Child safety scissors**
- **Large white paper plate**
- **Stapler**
- **Yarn and string**
- **Poster paint**
- **Paintbrushes**
- **White craft glue**

Finished Peek-a-Boo
Carnival Mask

Here's What You Do

1 Cover table with newspaper. Make a single cut from the outside edge of the paper plate into the center, then overlap edges and staple together to form a slight peak in the center.

2 Cut holes in the mask for eyes, then tie string on each side to hold mask in place.

3 Paint a face on the plate, then glue on yarn for hair. Let dry completely before wearing.

MORE BIG FUN!

★ Ask a grownup to help you string packing popcorn with a needle and thread to make a necklace to wear at your Carnival celebration.

Neighborhood

Ghostly Sponge Prints

There's a way to make a friendly ghost—
This is what you can do:
Take a sponge and pour some paint,
The rest is up to you!

Cut a ghost shape from a sponge.

Here's What You Need

- **Newspaper**
- **Poster paint (white)**
- **Heavy paper plate**
- **Sponge**
- **Child safety scissors**
- **Construction paper (dark color)**
- **Marker (black)**

Here's What You Do

1   Cover the table with newspaper, then pour a small amount of paint into the plate.

2   Cut a ghost shape from the sponge. Dip the sponge into paint, then press down onto paper to make a ghost print. Let dry completely, then use the marker to draw the ghost's eyes and mouth. Make lots of ghostly prints.

Dip sponge into paint, and print on paper.

Finished Ghostly
Sponge Prints

MORE BIG FUN!

★ If you carve a jack-o-lantern, save the pumpkin seeds. Wash them, dry them, and bake them in a 350°F (175°C) oven with a grownup's help. Yum!

★ Read *Bony Legs* by Joanna Cole.

Paper Bag Mail Pouch

The mail carrier brings letters—
Here's one from a friend:
"There's going to be a party,
So please, do attend!"

Here's What You Need

- **Large paper grocery bag**
- **Child safety scissors**
- **Stapler**
- **Markers**

Here's What You Do

1 Cut a 6" (15 cm) strip from the top of the bag, then fold in the bag's edge.

2 Fold over the strip, and staple it to the inside of the bag for a strap.

3 Decorate the mail pouch.

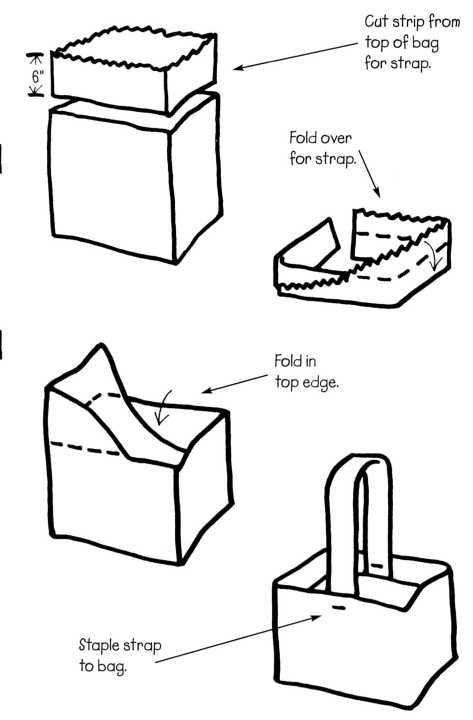

Cut strip from top of bag for strap.

Fold over for strap.

Fold in top edge.

Staple strap to bag.

Finished Paper
Bag Mail Pouch

MORE BIG FUN!

★ Did you ever get a letter in the mail? What did it say? Whom was it from?

★ Look in a world atlas to see where your stamps are from.

★ Ask your friends and relatives to save unusual stamps for you. Sort the stamps by the country they are from or by colors.

★ Cover a shoebox in recycled wrapping paper. Ask a grownup to cut a slit in the top, then use it for a mailbox.

Paper Plate Stop Sign

On your way to school each day,
There's someone that you meet—
The crossing guard tells you when
It's safe to cross the street!

Here's What You Need

- **Large white paper plate**
- **Child safety scissors**
- **Marker (black)**
- **Construction paper (red)**
- **White craft glue**
- **Stapler**
- **Cardboard paper towel tube**

Here's What You Do

1 Cut out an octagon (eight-sided shape) from the center of the plate, then trace the shape onto the construction paper.

2 Cut out the construction paper and glue onto the plate.

3 Use black marker to write the word *STOP* on the sign.

4 Staple the octagon onto the towel tube for a stop sign.

Cut octagon shape from paper plate.

Trace shape onto construction paper; cut out, and glue together.

Staple tube on bottom of sign.

Finished Paper
Plate Stop Sign

MORE BIG FUN!

★ Draw a picture of children walking between the white crossing lines to get to school.

★ Make up other signs. What might a sign look like that means *Don't Touch* or *Baby Sleeping*? Make some signs for your bedroom door.

★ Next time you're in the car, count how many stop signs you see. Why do you think stop signs are important to watch for?

Foil Mirror Headband

A pain, an ache, a bruise, a bump—
The doctor always knows
Exactly how to fix you up,
From your head to your toes!

Here's What You Need

- **Construction paper**
- **Child safety scissors**
- **Stapler**
- **Shirt cardboard**
- **Recycled aluminum foil**

Here's What You Do

1 Cut a band of construction paper 4" (10 cm) wide. Measure the length to fit around your head. Fold over, and staple ends together.

2 Cut a round shape from the cardboard, then wrap with foil. Staple it onto the front of the headband for a mirror.

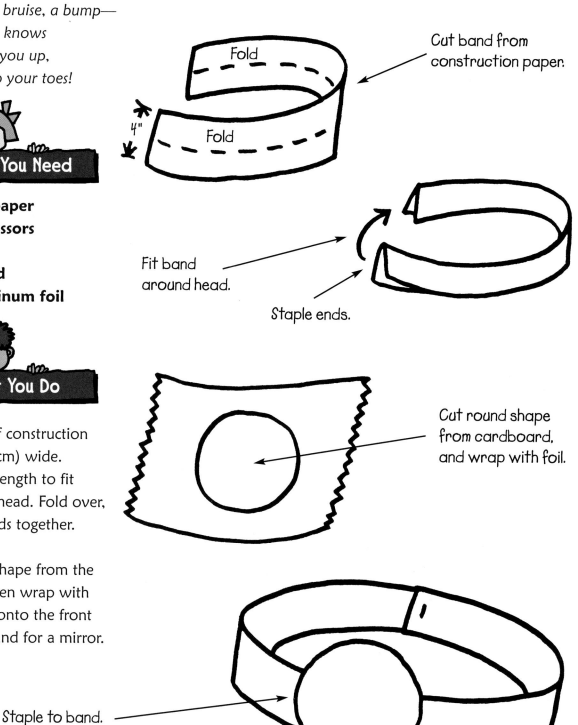

Fold

Fold

4"

Cut band from construction paper.

Fit band around head.

Staple ends.

Cut round shape from cardboard, and wrap with foil.

Staple to band.

Finished Foil
Mirror Headband

MORE BIG FUN!

★ Fill a shoebox with first-aid supplies such as ACE bandages, Band-Aids, cotton balls, sterile pads, surgical tape, resealable plastic bag (for ice packs), and alcohol swabs to keep in the closet or car.

★ Draw faces on tongue depressors for stick puppets. Glue on cotton balls for hair or beards.

★ Fill a small bag with crayons, paper, stickers, books, and playing cards. Take it with you to keep busy in the doctor's waiting room.

"Open Wide" Paper Bag Puppet

Your dentist takes care of your teeth
To keep them sparkling white;
But you must also do your part
And brush them every night!

Here's What You Need

- **Small brown paper bag**
- **Markers**
- **Construction paper (red and white)**
- **Child safety scissors**
- **White craft glue**

Here's What You Do

1. Draw the puppet's upper lip on the top flap of the bag, then draw the bottom lip on the bag just under the flap.

2. Cut the tongue and mouth from red construction paper, then glue them under the flap.

3. Cut out the puppet's eyes and teeth from white paper, then glue them onto the puppet.

Finished "Open Wide" Paper Bag Puppet

MORE BIG FUN!

★ Use an egg timer to time yourself when you're brushing your teeth.

Outdoor Fun

Cardboard Carton Obstacle Course

A tricycle has three small wheels;
Bicycles have two—
Whichever one you choose to ride,
Wear a helmet too!

Here's What You Need

- **Newspaper**
- **Poster paint**
- **Heavy paper plate**
- **Large paintbrush**
- **Large cardboard boxes**

Here's What You Do

1 Cover the floor with newspaper. Pour a small amount of paint into the paper plate. Paint the boxes. Let dry completely.

2 Place boxes in an obstacle course formation, then ride bicycles around them.

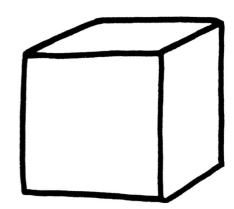

Finished
Cardboard
Carton Obstacle
Course

MORE BIG FUN!

★ Paint cartons with traffic signs such as Railroad Crossing, Steep Hill, Curves in Road, and Deer Crossing.

★ Decorate bikes with crepe-paper streamers for a parade on wheels.

★ Everyone tell one safe-biking rule.

Flashlight Fun

Camping out can be great fun,
Though you won't get much sleep;
Instead of telling stories,
You should be counting sheep!

Here's What You Need

- **Paper cup**
- **Pointed tool (pencil or pen point, nail—to be used only with a grownup's help)**
- **Flashlight**

Here's What You Do

1 Carefully poke holes in a design on the bottom of the cup.

2 In a dark room or tent, shine the flashlight into the cup to see a pattern of light on the wall or ceiling.

3 Use additional cups to make different patterns. Turn cups to get a kaleidoscopic effect.

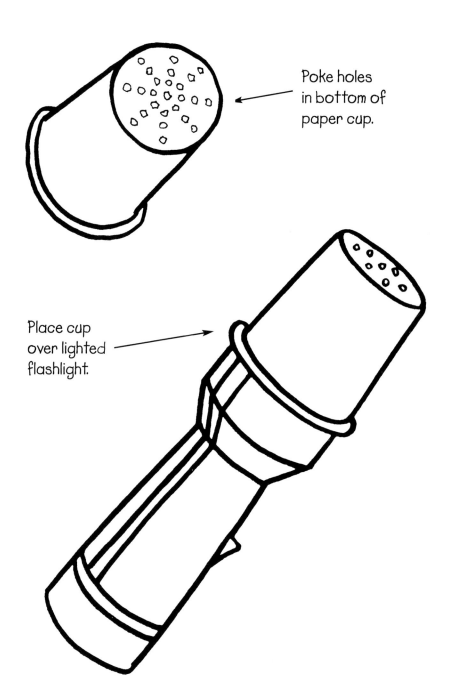

Poke holes in bottom of paper cup.

Place cup over lighted flashlight.

Flashlight Fun

MORE BIG FUN!

★ Look at the constellations on a clear night.

★ Cut out star shapes from recycled aluminum foil. Glue them onto black or dark blue construction paper for stars in a nighttime sky.

★ Make animals on the wall with flashlight shadows.

★ See who can tell the *funniest* joke, the *scariest* story, or the *silliest* rhyme.

Picnic Pack

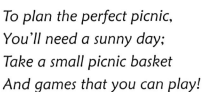

To plan the perfect picnic,
You'll need a sunny day;
Take a small picnic basket
And games that you can play!

Here's What You Need

- **2 large cereal boxes**
- **Child safety scissors**
- **Stapler**
- **White or brown shelf paper or recycled gift wrap**
- **Tape**
- **Yarn**
- **Markers**

Here's What You Do

1 Cut out one side panel from each cereal box. Slide boxes halfway inside each other, then staple boxes together to make a picnic pack.

2 Wrap boxes in shelf paper, then tape in place. Staple yarn onto sides of box for strap.

3 Decorate the picnic pack with markers, then pack it with plates, cups, napkins, and utensils.

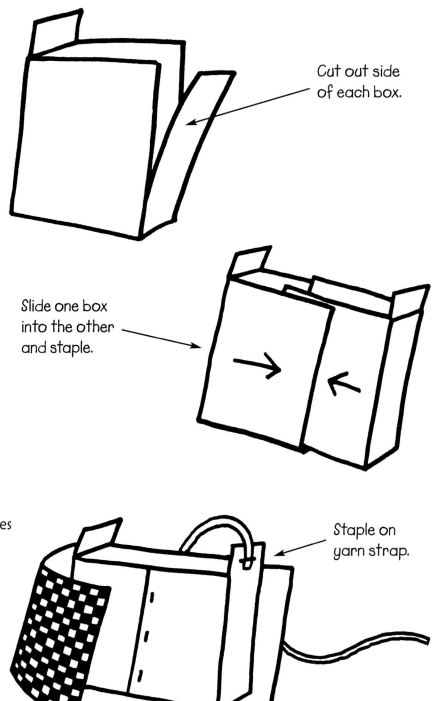

Cut out side of each box.

Slide one box into the other and staple.

Staple on yarn strap.

Cover with shelf paper and tape.

Finished
Picnic Pack

MORE BIG FUN!

★ Press raisins into cream cheese or peanut butter spread into a stalk of celery for an "ants on a log" picnic snack.

★ Read *Winter Picnic* by Robert Welber.

★ What would you eat and drink on a *winter* picnic? On a *summer* picnic?

Egg Carton Seed Starter

To start a little garden,
Plant a tiny seed;
Give it water every day,
And growth is guaranteed!

Here's What You Need

- **Egg carton**
- **Planting soil**
- **Seeds (flower or vegetable)**
- **Construction paper**
- **Child safety scissors**
- **Markers**
- **Popsicle sticks**
- **White craft glue**

Here's What You Do

1 Fill each section of the egg carton half full with soil, then plant seeds.

2 Cut construction paper into 3" (7.5 cm) squares.

3 Draw or write on paper squares to identify the seeds. Glue paper onto Popsicle sticks.

4 Place sticks in soil. Place seed starter in a sunny window, and water sparingly.

Fill egg sections half full of soil.

Push seeds into soil.

Cut square out of paper, then glue onto Popsicle stick.

RED RADISH

Decorate front of card.

Finished Egg
Carton Seed
Starter

LETTUCE   TOMATO

MORE BIG FUN!

★ Transplant the seedlings from the egg carton to a larger container or the garden.

★ Visit a nearby farmers' market, and see the different kinds of fruits and vegetables grown in your area.

★ Read *The Carrot Seed* by Ruth Krauss.

★ Look for tree seedlings before the lawn is mowed in the spring. Look for maple or elm tree seeds with bright green shoots close to the ground.

Bubble Prints

*It's fun to play in water
By floating things on top,
Or blow bubbles with a straw
And watch them go pop! pop!*

Here's What You Need

- **Newspaper**
- **Liquid dishwashing detergent**
- **Large bowl**
- **Water**
- **Food coloring**
- **Drinking straw**
- **White paper**

Here's What You Do

1 Work outdoors or cover a table with newspaper. Pour ¼ cup (50 ml) liquid dishwashing detergent into the bowl, then add a small amount of water and a few drops of food coloring.

2 Practice blowing out through a straw (don't suck in or you will get a mouthful of soap!). Blow into the bowl until bubbles rise to the top.

3 Gently lay a sheet of white paper over the bubbles to make a colorful bubble print.

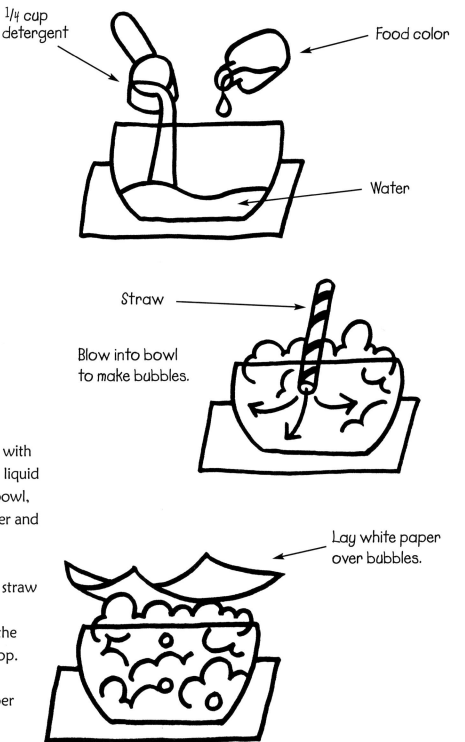

¼ cup detergent

Food color

Water

Straw

Blow into bowl to make bubbles.

Lay white paper over bubbles.

Finished
Bubble Prints

MORE BIG FUN!

★ Fill a bucket with water, and use a wide brush to "paint" outdoors. Watch as the drawing evaporates in the sun.

★ Shape pipe cleaners into wands. Mix together ¼ cup (50 ml) liquid dishwashing detergent, ¾ cup (175 ml) cold water, and

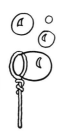

5 drops glycerin (available at a pharmacy). Dip wand in bubble mixture and blow.

★ What colors do you see in the bubbles? Where else have you seen those colors?

Rainbow Snow

Snow has fallen throughout the night
To make a place to play;
Put on your mittens, scarf, and boots,
And then get out your sleigh!

Here's What You Need

- **Bucket**
- **Water**
- **Food coloring**
- **Wide paintbrush**

Here's What You Do

1 Fill the bucket with water, then add a few drops of food coloring.

2 Use the brush to "paint" the snow.

Finished Rainbow Snow

MORE BIG FUN!

★ Look closely at freshly fallen snow. Do you see any animal tracks?

Big Fun in Special Places

The Zoo: Zany Zoo Animals

There's a place where people go
To see a kangaroo,
Lions, tigers, elephants—
All living at the zoo!

Here's What You Need

- **Shirt cardboard**
- **Pencil**
- **Child safety scissors**
- **Markers**
- **Poster paint**
- **Paintbrush**
- **Corrugated cardboard (from box or carton)**

Here's What You Do

1 Draw on shirt cardboard the shape of zoo animals with ½" (1 cm) tabs extending from the legs. Cut out, and decorate animals with markers.

2 Paint the corrugated cardboard and let dry completely.

3 Ask a grownup to cut small slits in the corrugated cardboard to fit tabs. Stand the animals upright in the slits.

Cut out animal shape.

Draw details with marker.

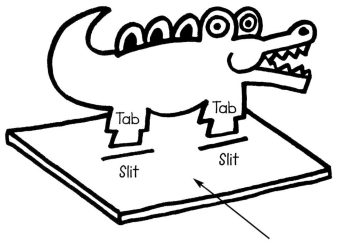

Insert tabs through slits in cardboard base.

Finished Zany
Zoo Animal

MORE BIG FUN!

★ Pick your favorite zoo animal, then *pretend* to be it. Can anyone guess what you are?

★ Write each letter of the alphabet on twenty-six sheets of paper, then draw a picture of an animal

(real or imaginary) whose name starts with that letter. Staple pages together to make an *alphabet animal book.*

★ No zoo near you? Visit a pet store instead.

The Museum: Fancy Frame

There's much to learn about the world,
And here's where you can start:
Museums exhibit artifacts,
Plus insects, gems, and art!

Here's What You Need

- **Ruler**
- **Artwork**
- **Cardboard**
- **Construction paper**
- **Child safety scissors**
- **White craft glue**
- **Small decorations (seeds, sequins, buttons, or ribbons)**
- **Sharp tool (for a grownup's use only)**
- **Yarn**

Here's What You Do

1 Measure the artwork, then cut cardboard and construction paper 2" (5 cm) larger on every side than the artwork.

2 Glue construction paper onto cardboard, then glue artwork in the center of the paper.

Glue paper onto cardboard.

Glue artwork in center of paper.

Thread yarn through holes.

Glue small decorations around artwork.

3 Glue small decorations around the artwork. Ask a grownup to make two holes in the top of the cardboard, then thread yarn through holes to hang.

Finished Fancy Frame

BYME

MORE BIG FUN!

★ Take a "Kids Like You Tour" at your local art museum. Find works of art that show children like you; then, when you get home, draw a self-portrait.

★ Do you like dolls or cars? Visit a doll museum or an antique car museum.

★ What's your favorite picture? Is it a *painting* on the wall? A *photo* in a frame? A *drawing* in a book?

The Circus: Straw Acrobat

A circus clown is silly,
Wearing such baggy clothes;
Those big feet make us giggle,
As does a bright red nose.

Here's What You Need

- **Construction paper**
- **Markers**
- **Child safety scissors**
- **Pipe cleaners**
- **Tape**
- **Drinking straws**

Here's What You Do

1 Draw the body of an acrobat on construction paper, then cut it out.

2 Tape pieces of pipe cleaner to the back of the acrobat for arms and legs. Draw acrobat's costume, face, and hair.

3 Bend pipe cleaner arms, and wrap them around the straw for a trapeze.

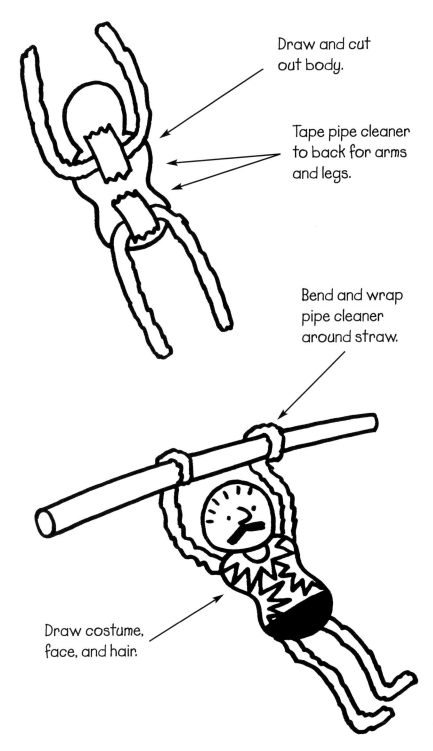

Draw and cut out body.

Tape pipe cleaner to back for arms and legs.

Bend and wrap pipe cleaner around straw.

Draw costume, face, and hair.

Finished Straw Acrobat

MORE BIG FUN!

★ Fold a 12" (30 cm) square paper in half diagonally. Turn the two points in to meet the third point, then tape in place to make a paper cone. Fill the cone with popcorn for a circus snack.

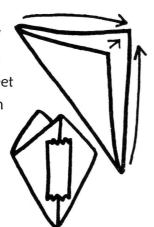

★ Dress up in big shoes, a long, wide tie, and silly pants. Plan a funny circus clown trick.

★ Have a somersault contest to see who can do the most somersaults in a row!

★ Read *The Magic Ring* by Hannah Machotka.

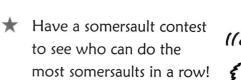

The Beach: Seashell Paperweight

At the beach you'll play in sand
Along the ocean shore;
Then search for fancy seashells—
There's so much to explore!

Here's What You Need

- **Newspaper**
- **Mixing stick**
- **Plaster of Paris**
- **Water**
- **Large disposable bowl**
- **Recycled margarine tub**
- **Seashells**
- **Poster paint**
- **Paintbrush**

Here's What You Do

Pour plaster into margarine tub.

Press shells into plaster.

1   Cover table with newspaper. Use stick to mix 1 cup (250 ml) plaster of Paris with water in the disposable bowl until the consistency of paste. Pour plaster into the margarine tub.

2   Press shells in plaster, and allow to harden completely.

3   Carefully remove plaster paperweight from tub. Decorate with poster paints, or leave natural.

Finished Seashell
Paperweight

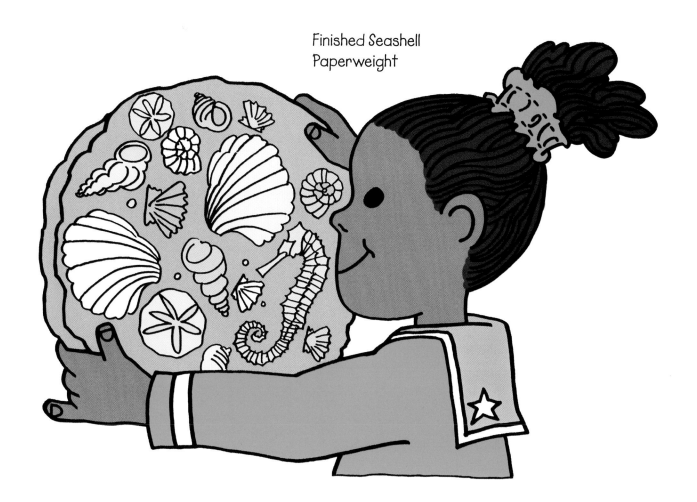

MORE BIG FUN!

★ Cover shirt cardboard with glue, then sprinkle on sand. Cut fish, sailboats, and a beach umbrella from construction paper; then glue onto cardboard to make a beach scene.

★ Put a seashell to your ear. Can you hear the sound of the ocean?

★ At the beach, collect shells. Once home, sort unusual shells for a collection. Save the rest for art and craft projects.

★ Close your eyes and touch some different seashells. Do they feel *smooth*? *Rough*? *Bumpy*? Are they *cool* or *warm*?

The Library: Photo Bookmark

If you're looking for adventure,
The library is near;
A book can take you 'round the world,
Without leaving your chair!

Here's What You Need

- **Construction paper**
- **Child safety scissors**
- **Old snapshots**
- **White craft glue**
- **Clear contact paper**
- **Hole punch**
- **Yarn**

Here's What You Do

1 Cut construction paper 6" x 2" (15 cm x 5 cm). Cut out pictures of family members from old snapshots, and glue onto construction paper to make a bookmark.

2 Cover the bookmark with contact paper, then trim edges.

3 Punch a hole in the top of the bookmark, thread yarn through, and knot to make a tassel.

Cut paper.

Glue on photo.

2"

6"

Apply contact paper, then trim.

Thread yarn through hole in top.

Finished Photo
Bookmark

MORE BIG FUN!

★ Ask friends and family to come to a "Book Swap Party." Have guests contribute books they can part with, then have them select a book to take home.

★ Glue pictures from recycled greeting cards onto 2" x 6" (5 cm x 15 cm) strips of construction paper to make bookmarks.

The Farm: Old MacDonald Mural

Farmers plow and plant and pick,
And some raise cattle too.
They work all day from dawn to dusk
Since there's so much to do!

Here's What You Need

- **Newspaper**
- **Poster paint (red and black)**
- **2 heavy paper plates**
- **2 sponges**
- **Child safety scissors**
- **Roll of shelf paper or butcher paper**
- **Markers**

Here's What You Do

1 Cover table with newspaper. Pour a small amount of red paint into a plate, then pour black paint into the other plate.

2 Cut one sponge in the shape of a triangle, then cut the other in the shape of a rectangle.

3 Dip the rectangular sponge into red paint, then press onto the roll of paper for the barn. Dip the triangular sponge in black paint and press onto paper on top of rectangle for the roof of the barn.

4 Draw things found on a farm, such as fences, pastures, gardens, cows, pigs, or horses.

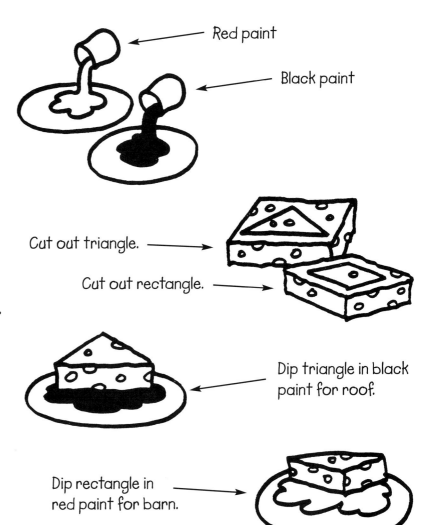

Red paint

Black paint

Cut out triangle.

Cut out rectangle.

Dip triangle in black paint for roof.

Dip rectangle in red paint for barn.

Finished Old MacDonald Mural

MORE BIG FUN!

★ Fill a clean jar halfway with whipping cream. Tighten lid and shake jar six minutes for whipped cream, then continue shaking for butter.

★ Visit a dairy farm. Learn how they milk cows *today*,  and how they milked cows in *earlier times*.

★ Would you like to live on a farm? What would be your favorite chore?

★ Read *Farmer Duck* by Martin Waddell.

The Aquarium: Paper Plate Fish Tank

When you go to aquariums,
There're many fish to see:
The octopus and sharks and eels,
The whales and manatee!

Here's What You Need

- **2 heavy paper plates**
- **Child safety scissors**
- **Plastic wrap**
- **Tape**
- **Construction paper (blue)**
- **Markers**
- **Recycled aluminum foil**
- **White craft glue**

Here's What You Do

1 Cut out the center of one plate, then tape plastic wrap across the opening.

2 Trace plate center onto blue construction paper, then cut it out. Glue it into the center of the second plate. Cut fish shapes from recycled aluminum foil, and glue onto blue paper.

3 Decorate fish, then tape plates together to make an aquarium.

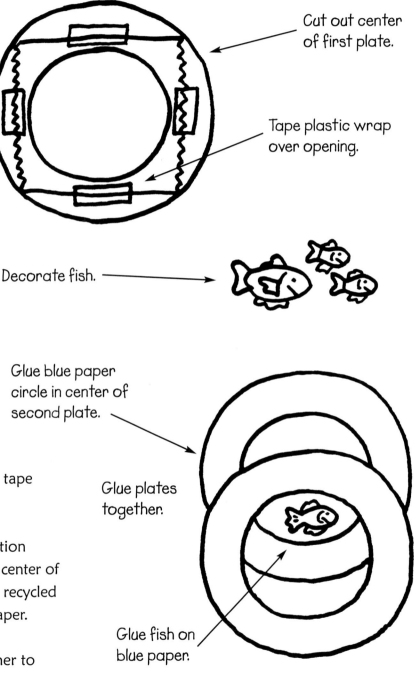

Cut out center of first plate.

Tape plastic wrap over opening.

Decorate fish.

Glue blue paper circle in center of second plate.

Glue plates together.

Glue fish on blue paper.

Finished Paper Plate Fish Tank

MORE BIG FUN!

★ Hang a string from a long pole, and attach a magnet to the end of the string. Cut out fish from construction paper, and put a paper clip on each one. Dangle the fishing line, and try to "catch" a fish.

★ Visit an aquarium or pet store. What is the main difference between freshwater and saltwater fish?

★ Read *The Magic Fish* by Freya Littledale.

Index

A

"All About Me" Scrapbook, 52–53
animals, zany zoo, 126–127
Apple Print Book Bag, 22–23

B

bags
    apple print book bag, 22–23
    paper, mail pouch, 106–107
    picnic, 118–119
    polka-dot lunch bag, 36
Berry Basket Cricket House, 98–99
boats
    bobbing, 40–41
    Tray Sailboat, 50
Bobbing Boat, 40–41
bookmark, photo, 134–135
books. *See* stories
bookshelves, cardboard box, 48–49
Bottle Bowling Pins, 38–39
bracelets, friendship, 72–73
Brown Bag Turkey, 74–75
Bubble Prints, 122–123
butter, make homemade, 137

C

candle, floating Diwali, 90–91
Cardboard Box Bookshelves, 48–49

Cardboard Carton Obstacle Course, 114–115
Cardboard Carton Storage Cart, 44–45
Cereal Counter, 30–31
clocks
    cookie sheet, 32–33
    types of, 33
collages
    "Love the Earth," 69
    nature, 13
Color Match Game, 26–27
color
    and feelings, 87
    bright/dark, 95
    in bubbles, 123
    matching game, 26–27
compare/contrast, 11, 50, 53, 55
Cookie Sheet Clock, 32–33
counting, 30–31, 33
Cozy Kitty Pillow, 62–63
Crackled Egg Art, 80–81

E

Earth Day Crown, 8–9
egg art, crackled, 80–81
Egg Carton Seed Starter, 120-121
emotions. *See* feelings

F

family tree, handprint, 54–55
Fancy Frames, 128–129
Fantastic Footprints, 14–15
feelings
    colors and, 87
    happy, 73
figures, straw, 130–131
fish tank, paper plate, 138–139
Flashlight Fun, 116–117
flavors, 36
Floating Diwali Candle, 90–91
Foil Mirror Headband, 110–111
Four Season Trees, 18
frame, Popsicle, 73
Friendship Bracelets, 72–73
Friendship Paper Quilt, 66–67

G

games
    bowling, 38–39
    color matching, 26–27
    shape matching, 27
    puzzle, picture, 46–47
Ghostly Sponge Prints, 104–105

H

Handprint Family Tree, 54–55
Happy Notepaper, 76
hats and headbands
    crown, award-winner's, 57
    crown, Earth Day, 8–9

foil mirror headband, 110–111

headband, Yankee Doodle
Dandy, 78–79

Vietnamese-style hat, 93

Hearts & Flowers Necklace,
58–59

holidays

Children's Day, 85

Diwali, 90–91

Fourth of July, 78–79

springtime, 81

Sukkoth, 83

Thanksgiving, 74–75

J

jewelry

bracelets, friendship, 72–73

necklace, hearts & flowers,
58–59

L

lantern, Vietnam swinging,
92–93

letters, 21, 24–25, 127

Love Plant, 68–69

lunch bag, polka-dot, 36

M

mailbox, homemade, 107

maraca, seed shaker, 100–101

masks

carnival, 102

dragon, paper bag, 86–87

medal, "We're So Proud!",
56–57

mobiles

boat, 41

sparkling shapes, 28–29

mural, old MacDonald,
136–137

N

nametag, noodle, 20–21

necklace, hearts & flowers,
58–59

Noodle Nametag, 20–21

notepaper, printing on, 76

O

Oatmeal Canister Drum, 88–89

obstacle course, cardboard
carton, 114–115

Old MacDonald Mural,
136–137

"Open Wide" Paper Bag
Puppet, 112

P

painting, footprint, 14–15

Paper Bag Dragon, 86–87

Paper Bag Mail Pouch, 106–107

Paper Plate Fish Tank, 138–139

Paper Plate Stop Sign, 108–109

paperweight, seashell, 132–133

Peek-a-Boo Carnival Mask, 102

Photo Bookmark, 134–135

Picnic Packs, 118–119

picture frames

fancy, 128–129

Popsicle stick, 73

Picture Puzzle, 46–47

Pie Tin Wind Chimes, 42–43

pillow, cozy kitty, 62–63

piñata, make a, 101

placemat, tea party, 70

Polka-Dot Lunch Bag, 36

pouch, tooth fairy, 63

Pressed Flower Card, 94

printing

apple, 22–23

bubble, 122–123

lunch bag, 36

notepaper, happy, 76

sponge, 96–97, 104–105

puppets

finger, stocking, 60–61

paper bag, "Open Wide,"
112

pet, sock puppet, 16–17

stick, 111

stocking, finger, 60–61

turkey, 75

puzzle, picture, 46–47

Q

quilt, paper friendship, 66–67

R

Rainbow Snow, 124

recycled art materials, 9

rubbings

leaf, 13

sandpaper letter, 24–25

S

Sandpaper Letter Rubbings, 24–25

Sawdust Bugs, 12–13

scrapbook, "All About Me," 52–53

sculpting, sawdust bugs, 12–13

sculpture

    brown bag turkey, 74–75

    love plant, 68–69

Seashell Paperweight, 132–133

seasons, 11, 18

Seed Shaker Maraca, 100–101

Sewing Card Tree, 10–11

shadow play, flashlight, 116–117

shapes

    hunting for, 29

    matching game, 27

    mobile, make a, 28–29

sign, paper plate, 108–109

sign language, learn some, 59

snow, rainbow, 124

Sock Puppet Pet, 16–17

sounds

    bowling alley, 39

    cricket, 99

    windy day, 43

Sparkling Shapes Mobile, 28–29

Stocking Finger Puppet, 60–61

stories

    Annabelle Swift, Kindergartner, 21

    Bedtime for Francis, 33

    Bony Legs, 105

    Carrot Seed, The, 121

    Chicka Chicka Boom Boom, 25

    Chin Chaing and the Dragon's Dance, 87

    Farmer Duck, 137

    Frog and Toad Are Friends, 73

    La La Salama, 89

    Magic Fish, The, 139

    Magic Ring, The, 131

    Picture Book of Martin Luther King Jr., A, 67

    Socks for Supper, 17

    Very Quiet Cricket, The, 99

    Winter Picnic, 119

Straw Acrobats, 130–131

stuffed paper fish, 84–85

sukkah, shoebox, 82–83

swinging lantern, 92–93

T

tea party placemat, 70–71

textures, 11, 25, 133

time, telling, 32–33

Tooth Fairy Pouch, 64

Tray Sailboat, 50

trees, 8–11, 13, 18

turkey, brown bag, 74–75

W

weather, 34–35

Weather Watch Board, 34–35

"We're So Proud!" Medal, 56–57

wind chimes, pie tin, 42–43

wind sock, 43

Y

Yankee Doodle Dandy Headband, 78–79

Z

Zany Zoo Animals, 126–127

More Good Books from Williamson Books

Williamson Books are available from your bookseller or directly from Ideals Publications.
Please see last page for contact and ordering information.

Little Hands® Books for Ages 2 to 7:

Parent's Guide Children's Media Award
Alphabet Art
With A to Z Animal Art
& Finger Plays
BY JUDY PRESS

Parents' Choice Recommended Award
Animal Habitats!
Learning About North American
Animals and Plants through Art,
Science, and Creative Play
BY JUDY PRESS

Around-the-World Art & Activities
Visiting the 7 Continents
through Craft Fun
BY JUDY PRESS

Art Starts for Little Hands!
Fun & Discoveries for
3- to 7-year-olds
BY JUDY PRESS

Creating Clever Castles & Cars
(From Boxes and Other Stuff)
Kids Ages 3–8 Make Their Own
Pretend Play Spaces
BY MARI RUTZ MITCHELL

Parents' Choice Gold Award
Fun with My 5 Senses
Activities to Build Learning Readiness
BY SARAH. A. WILLIAMSON

Kindergarten Success
Helping Children Excel
Right from the Start
BY JILL FRANKEL HAUSER

Parent's Guide Classic Award
LifeWorks Magazine Real Life Award
The Little Hands Art Book
Exploring Arts & Crafts
with 2- to 6-year-olds
BY JUDY PRESS
Parents' Choice Approved

Little Hands Create!
Art & Activities for Kids
Ages 3 to 6
BY MARY DOERFLER DALL

Parents' Choice Approved
Little Hands Paper Plate Crafts
Creative Art Fun for
3- to 7-Year-Olds
BY LAURA CHECK

American Bookseller Pick of the Lists
Math Play!
80 Ways to Count & Learn
BY DIANE MCGOWAN & MARK
SCHROOTEN

Science Play!
Beginning Discoveries for 2- to 6-Year-
Olds
BY JILL FRANKEL HAUSER

Sing! Play! Create!
Hands-On Learning for
3- to 7-Year-Olds
BY LISA BOSTON

Kids Can!® Books for Ages 7 to 14:

Parents' Choice Recommended
Making Amazing Art!
40 Activities Using the
7 Elements of Art Design
BY SANDI HENRY

**The Kids' Multicultural
Art Book**
Art & Craft Experiences
from Around the World
BY ALEXANDRA MICHAELS

Parents' Choice Approved
**The Kids' Multicultural
Craft Book**
35 Crafts from
Around the World
BY ROBERTA GOULD

Parents' Choice Approved
Skipping Stones Multicultural
  Honor Award
Benjamin Franklin Best
  Multicultural Book Award
**The Kids' Multicultural
Cookbook**
Food & Fun Around the World
BY DEANNA F. COOK

American Bookseller Pick of the Lists
Dr. Toy Best Vacation Product
Kids' Crazy Art Concoctions
50 Mysterious Mixtures
for Art & Craft Fun
BY JILL FRANKEL HAUSER

Parent's Guide Children's Media
  Award
Kids' Art Works!
Creating with Color,
Design, Texture & More
BY SANDI HENRY

American Bookseller Pick of the List
Oppenheim Toy Portfolio Best
  Book Award
Skipping Stones Nature & Ecology
  Honor Award
EcoArt!
Earth-Friendly Art & Craft
Experiences for 3- to 9-Year-Olds
BY LAURIE CARLSON

Using Color in Your Art
Choosing Colors for
Impact & Pizzazz
BY SANDI HENRY

Wordplay Café
Cool Codes, Priceless Puzzles &
Phantastic Phonetic Phun
BY MICHAEL KLINE

Kids Write!
Fantasy & Sci Fi, Mystery,
Autobiography, Adventure & More
BY REBECCA OLIEN

Visit Our Website!

To see what's new with Williamson Books and Ideals Publications and learn more about specific titles, visit our website at: www.idealsbooks.com

To Order Books:

You'll find Williamson Books at your favorite bookstore, or you can order directly from Ideals Publications. We accept Visa and MasterCard (please include the number and expiration date).

Order on our secure website:
www.idealsbooks.com

Toll-free phone orders with credit cards:
1-800-586-2572

Toll-free fax orders:
1-888-815-2759

Or send a check with your order to:
Ideals Publications
Williamson Books Orders
2630 Elm Hill Pike, Suite 100
Nashville, Tennessee 37214

Catalog request: web, mail, or phone

Please add $4.00 for postage for one book plus $1.00 for each additional book. Satisfaction is guaranteed or full refund without questions or quibbles.